Overcoming TEXTBOOK FATIGUE

ReLeah Cossett Lent

Overcoming TEXTBOOK FATIGUE

21st Century Tools to Revitalize Teaching and Learning

Foreword by Jay McTighe

ASCD | Alexandria, Virginia USA

ASCD®
1703 N. Beauregard St. • Alexandria, VA 22311-1714 USA
Phone: 800-933-2723 or 703-578-9600 • Fax: 703-575-5400
Website: www.ascd.org • E-mail: member@ascd.org
Author guidelines: www.ascd.org/write

Gene R. Carter, *Executive Director;* Ron Miletta, *Chief Program Development Officer;* Richard Papale, *Publisher;* Laura Lawson, *Acquisitions Editor;* Julie Houtz, *Director, Book Editing & Production;* Darcie Russell, *Editor;* Lindsey Smith, *Graphic Designer;* Mike Kalyan, *Production Manager;* Circle Graphics, Inc., *Typesetter*

ASCD Member Book, No. FY13-2 (Nov. 2012, PSI+). ASCD Member Books mail to Premium (P), Select (S), and Institutional Plus (I+) members on this schedule: Jan., PSI+; Feb., P; Apr., PSI+; May, P; July, PSI+; Aug., P; Sept., PSI+; Nov., PSI+; Dec., P. Select membership was formerly known as Comprehensive membership.

PAPERBACK ISBN: 978-1-4166-1472-2   ASCD product #113005
Also available as an e-book (see Books in Print for the ISBNs).

Quantity discounts: 10–49 copies, 10%; 50+ copies, 15%; for 1,000 or more copies, call 800-933-2723, ext. 5634, or 703-575-5634. For desk copies: www.ascd.org/deskcopy

Library of Congress Cataloging-in-Publication Data

Lent, ReLeah Cossett.
Overcoming textbook fatigue : 21st century tools to revitalize teaching and learning/ ReLeah Cossett Lent ; foreword by Jay McTighe.
p. cm.
Includes bibliographical references and index.
ISBN 978-1-4166-1472-2 (pbk. : alk. paper)
1. Textbooks–United States. 2. Active learning—United States. 3. Motivation in education—United States. I. Title.
LB3047.L46 2012
371.3'2–dc23

2012028749

22 21 20 19 18 17 16 15 14 13 12   1 2 3 4 5 6 7 8 9 10 11 12

Overcoming TEXTBOOK FATIGUE

21st Century Tools to Revitalize Teaching and Learning

Foreword

I began teaching in 1971. Back in the day, we didn't have state or national standards to guide our planning. But we had textbooks. I recall that during my first month on the job, my principal told me that he was required to observe new teachers at least one time during their first month, and scheduled a date to visit my classroom the following week. He asked me what topic I would be teaching along with the lesson objectives so that he would have a context for the observation. That was easy. I simply pulled out the teacher's edition of the textbook and showed him the topic and objectives for the next chapter. Indeed, I assumed that was my job. After all, the district had invested in textbooks and surely I was expected to use them. (My students and their parents expected that the textbooks would be used as well.) So, textbooks guided my teaching for the year.

I survived my first year and entered my second year, with a bit more experience and confidence. A few teachers on staff eschewed textbooks in a quest for "teachable moments" and relevance—remember, this was the 1970s—and I resonated with their intentions. I also appreciated the structure that textbooks afforded, however, so my teaching evolved to a blended model. In my classroom, I used the books as a base but would sometimes depart on improvisational curricular voyages to explore topics that seemed more interesting to my students and me.

A few years into my career, I was selected to work with a pilot program for gifted and talented students. The program was advertised as being differentiated, which at the time meant that it couldn't follow the regular curriculum. So, my colleagues and I abandoned traditional textbooks and set out to create our own enrichment program to challenge highly able students. Since this was before the days of the Internet, finding high-quality and coherent curricular materials was daunting. We did our best. With the clarity of hindsight, I admit that the units my colleagues and I designed ranged from brilliant and engaging to superficial and pointless. The experience gave me an appreciation for the coherence and intellectual integrity that a well-developed program affords, along with the recognition that a one-size-fits-all curriculum rarely does.

The educational landscape has changed dramatically since 1971. Established national and state standards and high-stakes accountability tests have shaped curricular priorities and influenced instructional practices. The never-ending knowledge explosion combined with instant accessibility of information via computers, tablets, and smart phones has conspired to make print materials immediately dated. Yet textbooks remain a seemingly permanent fixture in many schools.

Following stints as a resource teacher, program administrator, state education staffer, and director of a performance assessment consortium, I co-wrote *Understanding by Design* (UbD) with Grant Wiggins. In that book, we advocate a three-stage backward design process for planning curriculum. Stage 1 calls for clarity about desired results including established standards, desired understandings, and companion essential questions. Stage 2 specifies the needed and appropriate assessments to determine the extent to which learners have achieved the targeted outcomes. Stage 3 spells out the learning plan to achieve those desired learning results.

We found that this design process really helps to clarify the role of textbooks in teaching. As teachers work through the three stages, it becomes evident that covering the content in a textbook is not the desired result (Stage 1). Moreover, teachers recognize that not all of the assessments found in a textbook align with standards and other desired results (Stage 2). Finally, when developing lesson plans (Stage 3), the textbook is more likely to be viewed as a resource to help achieve targeted goals. Indeed, that is one of the key points of the book you are reading–textbooks are not inherently good or evil. Textbooks are resources and should be used thoughtfully and judiciously.

Overcoming Textbook Fatigue offers many suggestions for making the most of a textbook's strengths, along with guidance as to when and how to depart from it. I especially appreciate the fact that the advice is framed around an understanding of the learning process. The most practical and proven ways to use a textbook are as a means of

- preassessing and activating prior knowledge;
- engaging learners in meaningful collaboration;
- developing relevant and contextual vocabulary learning;
- cultivating before-, during-, and after-reading strategies;
- encouraging reading and writing to learn;
- upgrading assessments; and
- effectively differentiating learning.

Equally as valuable as the advice on how to effectively use textbooks are the book's cautionary notes about improper uses of textbooks (page-by-page coverage) and overt abuses (sticking to a rigid pacing guide irrespective of learning results).

As my colleague, Grant Wiggins, and I repeatedly proclaim, the textbook is a resource, *not* the syllabus. This book will enable you to enact that mantra and use textbooks intelligently. Your students will thank you!

Jay McTighe
McTighe and Associates

Acknowledgments

This book had a long history before it finally morphed into its final form. Lisa Luedeke, my friend and editor of one of my previous books, *Adolescents on the Edge,* was the first person who talked with me about textbook fatigue. Her insight and instinctive understanding of educational issues were pivotal in helping me clarify my thoughts and organize them into a coherent whole. From there, Anita Gildea, my editor at Heinemann, spent hours with me as we discussed what direction the book would take and, more important, who the audience would be. She supported my decision to bring this project to ASCD, where I felt the strong emphasis on learning communities would help me reach the widest audience. Laura Lawson at ASCD took over from there and worked her magic in helping me sharpen the lines of my impressionistic creation. Her encouragement, wisdom, and great listening skills helped me crystallize some issues that I had been struggling with from the beginning of the project. When the manuscript was turned over to my editor, Darcie Russell, the real fun began. Darcie, the most detail-oriented person I have ever known, unmixed my metaphors and tracked down every vaguely referenced source I had slipped into the book—all with a great deal of patience and humor. I am in awe of her!

The book could not have happened without the wonderful teachers and principals across the nation who generously shared their students and experiences with me. I am also grateful to Karen Walton at Fannin County School District, who provided textbooks for me as I did research. Perhaps my greatest debt of gratitude goes to the staff at South Hall Middle School and Da Vinci Academy in Gainesville, Georgia. Principal Paula Stubbs, literacy coach Paige Bagwell, and English teacher Teresa Haymore took time out of their very busy schedules to facilitate my visits and answer my never-ending questions. Thank you to Cindy White, Melissa Madsen, Sara Atwill, Ley Hathcock, Megan Lewis, and Kent Townley for their insight.

As with all my books, my husband, Bert, and my father, Don Cossett, read each chapter and, with their scientific minds, helped me see with new eyes. I value their love and input more than they will ever know.

Introduction

Textbooks as we know them have been around since the end of the 18th century, but if you compare Thomas Dilworth's *The Schoolmaster's Assistant, Being a Compendium of Arithmetic both Practical and Theoretical,* first published in 1773, to a contemporary algebra textbook, you will find few similarities (Dilworth, 1798). Back then, the content was delivered in a question and answer style, mostly for the purpose of memorization. Today, textbooks practically dance on the desk. Despite the evolution, the 21st century brings challenges that publishers could never have imagined twenty years ago, beginning with a ubiquitous source of information online accompanied by a generation of students more comfortable with tapping keys than turning pages. Textbooks are still a mainstay in most classrooms throughout the world, either in print or online, but smart teachers are learning how to use them as one of many resources for a burgeoning curriculum rather than as the single, authoritative source of information to be taught to students.

Contributors to Textbook Fatigue

As a consultant, I have the great fortune of spending a lot of time with teachers (and students) in various situations. It is through my experiences during these collaborations that I coined the term "textbook fatigue." Textbook fatigue is more than a "tired of textbooks" malaise. It is a weariness with the entire business of using textbooks and programs as curriculum guides, a hopelessness brought on by robotically following both the sequence outlined by textbook publishers and the activities they provide. It is a term that targets scripted programs and step-by-step teachers' manuals that dismiss individualization of schools, teachers, and students. I hope that this book will be an antidote to textbook fatigue and spark a renewed commitment to working within a community where staff and students embrace active, thoughtful, and relevant learning through a variety of resources and tools.

Fidelity to the Textbook

I began to think in terms of textbook fatigue when I was sitting at a tiny table in a tiny chair with 1st grade teachers who were also perched uncomfortably on chairs that looked as if they were straight from the doll house in the corner of the room. I will never understand how K–2 teachers manage to sit on chairs that are made for the bottoms of humans weighing less than forty pounds, but that's another issue entirely. On this day, we were talking about writing, and these teachers were telling me that they simply did not have time to incorporate writing into their curriculum. Being a former English teacher, this sounded like heresy to me, but I managed to remain relatively calm. "How can you *not* have your children write?" I asked.

"There just isn't enough time for everything in the textbook," explained the team leader, pointing in dismay to the large teacher's edition of their reading text.

"We're already going so fast that the kids aren't getting it," a first-year teacher said, nearly in tears. "I can't fit in one more thing."

"Then why don't you slow down," I asked, "and include what you know is important, like writing?" They looked at me as only primary teachers can look at someone who has had way more experience with adolescents than with children who do most of their writing with a crayon.

"We have to follow the program with fidelity," the team leader explained patiently.

Ah . . . fidelity. I was reminded of when a well-respected literacy expert called "fidelity" the new *F*-word. Thankfully, the principal walked into the room. We had a great conversation about fidelity, about having teachers use their own knowledge to make wise curricular choices, and about slowing down if the kids aren't getting it. These teachers are first-rate professionals who care very much for their students, but they and so many others have been convinced that following the prescribed program is somewhat akin to giving your child the entire course of antibiotics: missing one dose could sabotage the treatment.

Let me make clear that I understand the necessity of following a sequence for many topics, particularly those in science and math. Curriculum is all about organizing information so that it scaffolds deep learning. And one strength of most textbooks is that they are impeccably organized. The problem is that teachers are often left out of the curriculum loop and feel they must follow, often in a mechanical way, the teacher's edition as if it were handed down from on high. That's a real concern today, especially with the increasing emphasis on 21st century skills and Common Core State Standards. We need to have students analyze, synthesize, and use information rather than simply memorize it; skeptically evaluate sources instead of obediently accepting everything in print; and learn to work collaboratively to solve problems instead of only passing tests. Teachers (whole schools, actually) must be actively involved in the planning, implementation, and evaluation of all phases of the curriculum, not obedient followers of a packaged textbook series.

So, using textbooks *as well as* a wide variety of supplemental resources to support effective instruction is what modern schooling is all about. Driving instruction from the textbook's table of contents or trying to cover everything in the text is actually counterproductive in that it distracts us from our most important task: helping students to internalize, apply, and transfer new learning in ways that are fresh and meaningful.

Insufficient Background Knowledge and Volume of Information

We have all experienced textbook fatigue and we've seen students suffer from it as well. The symptoms are obvious: we hide out in the teachers' lounge during textbook adoption, our students moan audibly when we ask them to open their texts, and we all try to figure out ways of transporting textbooks without risking permanent back injury.

In truth, textbook fatigue of both online and print texts may occur most often for students because they have insufficient background knowledge or vocabulary to help them make necessary connections with the many topics presented, invoking the "this is boring" chorus teachers hear every day. Texts are also sometimes written in a "just the facts, ma'am" style that is not especially interesting to students or doesn't come at the material from their perspective. In addition, because of the sheer volume of information contained within the pages of the text as well as the overwhelming array of supplemental materials, students often don't have time to assimilate a concept before being rushed to the next.

A similar scenario plagues teachers. Teacher editions are bulging with the latest reading strategies, online resources, coaching tips, graphic organizers, vocabulary instruction—as well as pages (and screens) of color-coded benchmarks, standards, and curriculum alignment. This material might be helpful if teachers had a few extra years to read it; instead, every few years teachers face a new textbook adoption that is more complex, more all-encompassing, more daunting than the last.

One Size Fits All

One of the reasons that textbooks and their associated resources weigh so much is that they are created to meet the needs of as many states, districts, teachers, and students as possible, which makes it a one-size-fits-all product. Larger states such as Florida, Texas, and California get the most attention, not because those states have more worthy students and teachers, but because they have more students and therefore more money to spend on textbooks. And lest we forget, all textbook publishers are for-profit businesses, in fact, multibillion-dollar businesses. Publishers spend millions keeping up with standards as well as with trends in education and often change their content when the political or educational winds shift. They use focus groups to report back to their marketing departments in much the same way that cereal companies survey their target audience to find out how much fiber they should put in their flakes.

Certainly, the individuals working for publishers may care about students and teachers, but the bottom line is sales. And if an idea isn't profitable, however engaging or commonsensical it may be, you won't see it in programs, textbook series, or supplemental resources.

Similarly, if a controversial topic such as the advantages of stem cell research in science or sexual content in literature (even Shakespeare) is questioned publicly by large groups of people, it is often soft-pedaled or omitted entirely. And if you think textbooks aren't political, think again. A significant example was highlighted in the *New York Times* in March 2010. "After three days of turbulent meetings, the Texas Board of Education on Friday approved a social studies curriculum that will put a conservative stamp on history and economics textbooks, stressing the superiority of American capitalism, questioning the Founding Fathers' commitment to a purely secular government and presenting Republican political philosophies in a more positive light" (McKinley, 2010). At the same meeting, "Efforts by Hispanic board members to include more Latino figures as role models for the state's large Hispanic population were consistently defeated" (McKinley, 2010).

The Washington Post covered the story as well, writing that "Historians on Tuesday criticized proposed revisions to the Texas social studies curriculum, saying that many of the changes are historically inaccurate and that they would affect textbooks and classrooms far beyond the state's borders." They explained that because the "Texas textbook market is so large, books assigned to the state's 4.7 million students often rocket to the top of the market, decreasing costs for other school districts and leading them to buy the same materials" (Birnbaum, 2010). This unfortunate occurrence supports the argument that textbooks should not be used as a single source of information, much less as a sole curriculum.

Perhaps more than anything else, textbooks are victims of the 21st century. With information doubling every two years, the vast textbook machine can't rumble along quickly enough. Editors begin working on print textbooks several years before publication; by the time the textbooks are published, much of the information may be stale if not completely wrong, especially in science. With so much information being generated by a global, digital world that never sleeps, editors must go crazy trying to determine what to include and what to discard.

That's not to say that there aren't some exemplary textbooks out there, but it's important to remember that textbooks were never intended to replace teachers' expertise, knowledge, or intuition in the classroom. Textbooks are simply a resource, a convenient way to allow students to have access to the same information at the same time, with suggestions from educational experts on how to use the information with students. Even as more schools are buying laptops or iPads and textbooks are moving into the online market, it's *how* we use these digital textbooks that will make the difference in students' learning. Using any online textbook as the only source of information ironically ignores the advantages inherent in electronic media, specifically the availability of high-quality (and often free) online articles, websites, and other open-source materials. What's more, text that is difficult to read doesn't become easier just because it is electronic.

How We Use Textbooks

In the United States, there is hardly a standard textbook use policy. When consulting in a large district in Kentucky, for example, the curriculum director told me that when administrators conduct walk-throughs, a teacher is "marked down" if she is using the textbook as a curriculum guide instead of as a resource. In another state, the district superintendent laughingly told me that she couldn't pry teachers' fingers from the textbooks—and then admitted that because of budget cutbacks they had few other additional resources. In several schools I've visited, teachers had only a few textbooks because they were expected to work together to create lessons from a variety of sources. In a small southern district, a gifted grant writer was able to procure iPads for each teacher; her next goal was to make them available to students so they could switch from print textbooks to an online version.

I've been in schools that have only classroom sets of textbooks and others with policies that require that each student be assigned a textbook. In one school, each teacher had a classroom set and each student had a stay-at-home textbook. Although the cost was exorbitant, administrators cut back in other areas because they felt print textbook access was a critical component of their literacy goals.

Textbook use is as varied as schools themselves, but what I am advocating is changing the way we use *all* textbooks, both print and online, by cultivating teachers' knowledge and experience rather than sublimating their abilities to textbooks and programs.

How to Revitalize Learning

One of the goals of this book, besides revitalizing learning for students as well as for teachers, is to show how communal learning can be commonplace throughout the school. Although it is possible for teachers to make the move from a textbook-centered curriculum to a resource-infused curriculum individually, it is much more difficult without the support of a group of colleagues to help fashion this change.

Linda Darling-Hammond, in her eye-opening book *The Flat World and Education,* examines why high-performing nations such as Finland, which she calls a "poster child for school improvement since it rapidly climbed to the top of the international rankings," are doing so much better than the United States on international tests (2010a, p. 164).

"In Finland, like other high performing nations, schools provide time for regular collaboration among teachers on issues of instruction." This collaboration is in the form of "powerful learning environments that continually improve as they learn to engage in a 'cycle of self-responsible planning, action and reflection/evaluation' " (2010a, pp. 172–173). She goes on to point out that this shift in teachers' learning has an effect on classroom practices. Teachers who engage in a cycle of planning, action, and reflection discover the challenges and rewards in what they expect their own students to do.

How much professional development in the United States is devoted to planning, action, and reflection/evaluation? As Yvette Jackson wrote in *The Washington Post,* "Much of the professional development teachers are required to attend is attached to textbook adoptions, mandates, or scripted programs that promise results that are rarely delivered" (2011). It seems that textbook fatigue is also plaguing professional development.

Communities of Reflection and Practice

The advantages of professional learning communities (PLCs) are well documented, but, unfortunately, many PLCs exist in name only, especially when schools do not commit the time necessary to make them successful. Often, PLCs are hurried affairs that focus on checklists and protocols, leaving members little energy for reflecting on student work and teaching practices. These groups have become, in too many schools, one more thing to add to teachers' (and administrators') long and burdensome days rather than a place where collaborative planning makes their work more interesting and productive. Sadly, the acronym PLC does not always invoke a positive response from teachers.

I like what the National Council of Teachers of English (NCTE) calls these PLCs: Communities of Practice. NCTE cites the following as characteristics of these communities:

- Connection to something larger
- Coordinated perspectives, discourse, and actions

- Shared resources to address recurring problems of practice concerning student learning
- Making visible tacit knowledge or learning (NCTE, 2011).

One of the best ways to overcome textbook fatigue is by forming such communities, either by grade level, content area, or in interdisciplinary teams. Another option is to work with a co-teacher. If you want help with starting or continuing group learning, note the Community of Practice section at the end of Chapters 1 through 7. These sections are designed to help you capitalize on the informal and formal benefits of peer collaboration and explore concepts presented in the chapter. It is the wisdom of your own crowd, at your own school, that will transform what may have been a PLC in name only into a vibrant working community.

Daniel Pink says that "Human beings have an innate inner drive to be autonomous, self-determined, and connected to one another" (2011, p. 73). He contends that when those conditions are met, there is really no limit to what can be accomplished. In this era of standardization and scripted curricula, we need to reembrace autonomy, self-efficacy, and relationships before we even touch the cover of our textbooks. Through interdependence, especially within our communities of learning, we can make wise decisions about how to use textbooks as resources to support instruction.

The National Commission on Teaching and America's Future pinpoints the challenge: "If America is to meet the needs of 21st century learners, we must move away from the norms that governed factory-era schools. . . . Transforming schools into 21st century learning communities means recognizing that teachers must become members of a growing network of shared expertise" (Fulton, Yoon, & Lee, 2005, p. 1). Teachers already have the shared expertise, or they can certainly grow it through study and collaboration, but they need *time* to examine appropriate text, plan lessons, and discuss how to engage students in learning if we want to see schools move solidly into the 21st century.

Resources for Revitalizing Learning

By relying on communities of learning, both in classrooms and within faculties, the chapters in this book will help teachers choose textbook activities wisely, assist students as they unlock difficult text, and find appropriate supplemental resources.

- Chapters 1, 3, and 4 address how to help students engage in deep, meaningful reading of all texts;
- Chapter 2 focuses on how to build background information;
- Chapter 5 shows how to incorporate writing into content-area study;
- Chapter 6 provides suggestions for using assessments that guide instruction;
- Chapter 7 offers advice on building text sets for all subject areas; and
- Chapter 8 gives a picture of schools that are already using textbooks as resources.

Overcoming Textbook Fatigue

This is a book about how to manage your textbook before it overtakes you, reclaim your curriculum from the table of contents, and embrace teaching as a joyful activity, not one driven by textbook demands. Those goals may sound nearly impossible, but I have seen entire schools delivered from textbook fatigue when given the support to work collaboratively on what their students need, not what textbook publishers decide their students need. This means reaching within *and* beyond the textbook to access all sorts of 21st century tools, the same ones that students will be using in college, their careers, and daily life. Just as we have moved on from the encyclopedia salesman who convinced us that no home was intellectually safe without a set of World Books, it is now obsolete to believe that there is one set of textbooks that can meet the needs of this generation of info-savvy kids.

1

Learning: It's All About Engagement

Sometimes referred to collectively as Generation M, *M* standing for media multitaskers, our students are adept at dealing with multiple stimuli, especially when the stimuli emanate from electronic devices. Not only do they enjoy multitasking, but these natives to the digital world often become impatient with those of us who have to consult the user's manual before activating our electronic gadgets.

Never before have students' lives outside of school been so different from their lives inside the classroom. This generation of students seldom chooses to use paper and pencil; the students' world revolves around visual images, and social networking is not a hobby but a way of life. In fact, Richard Restak in *The New Brain* notes that the plasticity of our brains responds to the technology all around us. "Our brain literally changes its organization and functioning to accommodate the abundance of stimulation forced on it by the modern world" (2003, p. 38).

Generation M, transported from the womb into a world of technology, tends to shut down when a teacher stands in front of the classroom and lectures using a dry PowerPoint presentation or when she tells students to read a chapter in the textbook and answer the questions. Today's students need to be actively learning, solving problems, and adapting information to meaningful tasks, all of which creates an engaging multimedia environment that draws students into the content rather than a textbook-fatigued environment that requires educators and parents to push kids from behind.

So how does engagement bridge the gap between our techie students and textbook fatigue? Prea Naick, a high school science teacher in North Carolina, knows a few things about engaging students in the text. I watched her students, in groups of three, create a vocabulary graphic organizer for the words from the textbook using the following prompts:

- What does it do?
- What are its benefits?
- What are its problems?
- What would happen if it did not occur?
- Illustrate it.

The students had limited time before presenting their organizers to the class, so they were busily engaged in the task, using their textbooks as a reference. Ms. Naick moved from group to group asking questions, providing additional information, and offering encouragement. One young man called her to his group, where he was in charge of drawing a picture of a lipid bilayer. He had copied an illustration from the text onto the organizer but didn't fully understand the drawing. Knowing that he would be required to explain it to the class and that both Ms. Naick and classmates might ask questions, he wanted a thorough understanding of the term. The teacher gave a clear explanation and he listened intently. After the group's presentation Ms. Naick asked him if he was sure that he got it; he nodded and gave a thumbs up sign. During each presentation, the other students took notes in the vocabulary section of their learning logs.

I can't help but compare Ms. Naick's class with my visit to another teacher's class. This second teacher was a knowledgeable middle school science teacher who stood in front of her class to offer an efficient presentation of cell division, while directing students to follow the lecture in their texts. In contrast to Ms. Naick's students who were actively involved in finding and applying information, the second teacher's students were sitting passively. At least one student was reading a novel that was cleverly hidden inside the science book, which was standing up on her desk.

Why Does Engagement Matter?

A few decades ago, engagement was not a term used in conference sessions, in professional book titles, or in most classrooms. Teachers taught, students followed instructions, and if engagement was part of the equation, so much the better. Students who were diligent and compliant generally passed the course. And if someone didn't pass, it was hardly the teacher's fault. Now with a focus on drop-out rates, especially in the United States where graduation rates are lower than in many other countries (OECD, 2011), engagement seems to be the new buzz word. Books, articles, and research extoll its benefits.

Guthrie and Wigfield (2000), for example, found students' engagement in subject-matter reading to be the *mediating* factor in improved student outcomes. More recently, John Guthrie made an even stronger case:

> Reading engagement and reading achievement interact in a spiral. Higher achievers read more, and the more engaged those students become the higher they achieve. Likewise, lower achievers read less, and the less engaged decline in achievement. The spiral goes downward as well as upward. In fact, continued low engagement is a precursor to dropping out of school." (2008, p. 3)

Brozo, Shiel, and Topping report that engagement in reading had the third largest impact on performance (after grade and immigration status). "Keeping students engaged in reading and learning might make it possible for them to overcome what might otherwise be insuperable barriers to academic success" (2007, p. 308). If we want students to achieve in all content areas, engagement is critical.

What Does Engagement Look Like?

I can feel the energy in an engaged classroom. In such classes, the textbook is seldom the center of the learning universe. Instead, the students' quest for understanding guides the process. The textbook or Internet may be a necessary component, but the content alone is powerless without an engaged learner. Allan Collins and Richard Halverson talk about just-in-time learning, a term that means "whenever you need to learn something in order to accomplish a task, you can find out what you need to know" (2009, p. 14). We have all experienced that phenomenon. We avidly read a sports story when our team is playing, we read every word of an insurance policy when a storm has damaged our roof, and we find the perfect recipe online for our Saturday night party. Engagement turns any text from a boring treatise into something that is alive with the possibility of finding what we need to know. Ms. Naick's student needed just-in-time learning about lipid bilayers, and when the text couldn't meet that need, he turned to another source. Too many students read the text without any sense of needing to know; they find enough information to satisfy the teacher or to fill in the blank on the worksheet and continue to the next page, unengaged and more convinced than ever that the content is boring.

How is it possible to instill curiosity for learning, that bright spark that permeates some classrooms? More important, how do we engage students in texts that they may find irrelevant or boring? There are no easy answers, but John Guthrie's model for engagement in reading is a great place to start. See Figure 1.1 for help.

1.1 Guthrie's Model for Engagement in Reading

Principle of Engagement	Description of Principle	Classroom Practices
Set Mastery Goals	Students want to reach goals for intrinsic under-standing rather than for a grade or reward.	• Make tasks relevant. • Use hands-on activities. • Provide reteach opportunities. • Reward effort over performance.
Provide Students with Control and Choice	Students take ownership over their reading	• Provide options for how to learn. • Give students input into curriculum. • Allow students to select knowledge displays. • Include inquiry projects.
Infuse Social Interaction	Students work collaboratively	• Allow student-led and open discussions. • Provide time for collaborative reasoning. • Relate to students as individuals. • Develop partnerships. • Scaffold social motivations over time.
Encourage Self-Efficacy	Students believe they can read and are determined to succeed.	• Recognize gaps between students and texts. • Locate texts matched to students' abilities. • Build confidence through goal-setting.
Cultivate Interest	Students feel that the text or topic is appealing	• Make real-world connections. • Extend intrinsic interests. • Create self-expressing and puzzling tasks.

Source: From *Engaging Adolescents in Reading* (pp. 133–134), by J.T. Guthrie (Ed.), 2008. Thousand Oaks, CA: Corwin. Adapted by permission.

As teachers, we all want to promote intrinsic motivation so students *want* to know more about the topics we are teaching, but there is much truth in the saying about leading a horse to water. Unfortunately, we've all seen a lot of horses that simply aren't thirsty. This chapter will provide a variety of practices for engaging students in learning from texts as well as from each other.

Engagement Through Mastery Goals

Mastery goals are not the same as performance goals, which often are the predominant goals in schools. Daniel Pink offers this distinction: "Getting an *A* in French class is a performance goal; being able to speak French is a learning goal" (2011, pp. 121–122). A mastery goal for a student in middle or high school studying vectors in algebra, for example, would be that she wants to understand the concept deeply if she aspires to go to college and major in engineering. A performance goal would be that the student completes an assignment to get a good grade; she may not care whether she understands the concept as long as she passes the test.

In an elementary math class, the first activity of the day for Christy Adams's 3rd and 4th graders was to vote on their favorite *something* (might be a soft drink, animal, holiday, or color). Then, Ms. Adams showed them how to make fractions based on the voting results. The students wanted to understand fractions because they were interested in seeing how their own preferences stacked up against their classmates' favorites. The teacher successfully helped students acquire mastery goals for learning fractions.

Douglass and Guthrie reported on a study where the researchers found that "Teachers who promoted performance goals had students who reported high levels of boredom, a lack of joy, and disinterest in their daily lessons" (2008, p. 24). Any time we can change performance goals into mastery goals, our chances of engaging students and increasing their understanding of our content are greater.

Mastery Goals and Relevance

What we believe about the nature of our abilities, or "self-theories," as Daniel Pink (2011) calls them, has everything to do with mastery; just as self-efficacy, our beliefs about our abilities to succeed at a task, has everything to do with engagement. When students develop a mastery mindset and believe they can accomplish a task because it matters to them, they are setting their own learning boundaries and will often exceed our goals for them. Student engagement boils down to this question: "Why does learning this content matter?" or in student vernacular, "Why do we have to do this?" Students have a right to know the answer. To ensure that you can answer their questions, think through the following before you begin any topic or chapter and share your answers with your students.

- How is this particular topic, information, or chapter relevant to this group of students?
- Why does this topic, information, or chapter matter?
- How can this information be used by my students?
- What connections can I make from this topic to students' lives, interests, or needs?

Engagement Through Control and Choice

Pink contends that three factors contribute to motivation when learning: autonomy, purpose, and mastery. If we think of autonomy as the opposite of being controlled, we can see how it would look in our classrooms. In the traditional classroom the teacher is in control of everything: the content, the method of delivery, the assessment, the seating arrangement, the type of materials to be used, the amount of social interaction, and perhaps even the temperature of the room. Pink renames autonomy "self-direction," a characteristic necessary for 21st century learners. "It [autonomy] means acting with choice—which means we can be both autonomous and happily interdependent with others" (2011, p. 90). And, he points out,

> Autonomy has a powerful effect on individual performance and attitude. According to a cluster of recent behavior science studies . . . autonomous motivation promotes greater conceptual understanding, better grades, enhanced persistence at school and in sporting activities, higher

> productivity, less burnout, and greater levels of psychological well-being. (2011, p. 90–91)

The students in Ms. Naick's class may not have had autonomy over everything, but they could make choices about the kind of graphic organizers they wanted to use and how they presented their charts. Providing choice as often as possible in terms of content, tasks, texts, partners, delivery, due dates, or assessment may be the key to engaging students, especially for those who have become disconnected with and disinterested in the content.

For those of us who are habitual control freaks, take it a step at a time. Perhaps start by allowing students to do just one of the following:

- Select a section of the text to read and then jigsaw what they learned.
- Choose from various assessment formats the one that they feel will best demonstrate their knowledge.
- Choose supplemental text (books, articles, websites) related to the topic and use class time to engage them in reading the materials.
- Take turns providing a prompt for journal writing or a word problem related to the topic. (See Chapter 5 for more information about journals.)
- Choose among various graphic organizers or note-taking strategies and use the one that makes the most sense to them.
- Use class time to finish reading, complete an assignment, or talk to a classmate about the topic. As students complete their assignments, allow them to choose among activities such as working on a writing assignment for their portfolio, reading a book related to the topic, or doing online research.
- Find an example in the text (or in real life) to support an inference or fact.

• Write questions they would like to ask about the chapter or topic.

• Choose due dates for assignments, especially projects; supply written excuse if they can't make the deadline. (See Chapter 6 for more information about redoing assignments.)

Fillman and Guthrie wrote about a math teacher who was frustrated because his students did not complete word problems, even when he assigned only half a page. He finally gave them the option of completing either the odd items or the even items at the end of one chapter. "Ninety percent of the students completed the homework. Remarkably, many students read all of the problems to decide which ones were the easiest. Then, after doing them all, they handed in the half on which they thought they did best" (2008, pp. 38–39). Choice may well be the silver bullet for engagement in text.

Engaging Students Through Social Interaction

If there is one change that you make in your instructional practice, I advocate for more collaborative learning. Just as the highest performing nations give teachers time to work together to reflect upon and improve their practice, students who are given time to work together vastly improve their learning. Harvey and Daniels cite studies that show "When students worked in small groups, taking significant responsibility for planning, undertaking, and reporting on research into subject matter, most scored significantly higher on content-area tests of math, history, literature, science, geography, and reading comprehension" (2009, p. 43). Perhaps one reason that they scored higher was that they were engaged in what they were learning.

The model of students sitting in rows so they don't talk to peers while listening to the teacher impart information is not only obsolete but damaging. Students in such classes report a lack of interest in subject matter and decreased motivation to learn more than is required for a passing grade. Today's students need to be actively working together to find and use information or solve problems. Steven Wolk makes the point that "Telling our students to sit quietly and listen will not turn them into lifelong learners or engaged citizens" (2008, p. 115). Today's students need to be learning *with others*.

There are two prongs to the concept of engagement through social interaction. One is collaborative learning, which is the natural result of having students solve problems together or engage in inquiry learning, perhaps in the form of web quests or experiments that begin with essential questions (see Chapters 4 and 8). The other is the act itself of social engagement—the wisdom and synergy that comes from being part of a group with a common goal or task. Think about a time when you went to a meeting or an event because you were mildly interested in the topic. For example, my husband and I went to an organizational meeting of a group that was forming to help with hunger in our area by growing community gardens. My husband is interested in gardening, but it's never been a passion of mine. Now, three years later, I am chair of the public relations committee and co-editor of the group's newsletter. Why? Social engagement. My interest in gardening has not increased, but the people in this group have become like family, and I wouldn't miss a meeting for anything. That is the kind of community that I recommend in classrooms—a place where students might not be fascinated with the content; in fact, they may even struggle with it as I do with gardening, but they show up and continue showing up because, like other social creatures, they enjoy being part of a close-knit group that works together.

It's not just a nice idea. Katherine Wentzel (1998) found that when students' social goals were met in a classroom, they had an increased desire to learn, get good grades, behave acceptably, and pursue academic performance. I have witnessed that such an approach goes a long way toward creating tolerance and reducing bullying in classrooms and schools. It's hard to pick on someone once you truly get to know him—his strengths and differences, aspirations and goals, insecurities and fears. There is really no downside to collaborative learning for students.

How to Create a Sense of Belonging

Students feel that they belong when they have a role or task in a group. Think about teams (or committees in upper grades) you could create in your own discipline. Every student would belong to at least one group in addition to working in other groups on content tasks. Following are examples of some standing committees you could form within classrooms.

Create a current events team that will scour *Time, Newsweek, USA Today* (online or in print) and bring to class any news they find that relates to the topic of study—or a previous topic of study. For example, when scientists determined that Pluto was not a planet, the science class's current events team was all over that news, providing articles to place on a bulletin board and sharing the new development orally with the class. The same was true for when Osama Bin Laden and Moammar Kadafi were killed—important historical events that won't appear in print textbooks for years.

Form a writing team in upper elementary or middle school that assists students with writing assignments by offering help with introductions, conclusions, or organization. In an English language arts class, for example, this may be specialized to a spelling team (those who are naturally good spellers), a comma team who "gets" the comma rules, or a vocabulary team. In science class, this could be a team that helps students with the scientific method and with the writing of lab reports.

Create a social team at any grade level. These students often make lists of birthdays and remind the class to honor that student on her special day. One high school class selected secret pals to make sure everyone felt special to at least one other person in the class. None of these activities interfered with instructional time but, rather, enhanced the learning through a positive and caring climate.

Devise other special teams that are dependent upon the content or topic of study: art teams, technology teams, book teams, logistics teams (the latter may be for passing out papers or turning on computers).

Once you turn ownership of the class over to its occupants, there are almost no limits to the benefits.

Minicollaborations

In traditional classrooms, the teacher asks a question and either acknowledges a student whose hand is raised or calls on a student who is trying to hide behind the textbook. In either case, once the teacher gives permission for this one student to answer, the rest of the class is simply off the hook. They can safely take their brains elsewhere—to the beach, to the argument they had with a friend that morning, to what they plan to eat for lunch—because their classmate is on the hot seat for at least several minutes with the undivided attention of the teacher.

One of the best ways to engage students in social interaction *and* overcome textbook fatigue is through a well-known strategy developed by Frank Lyman (1981) called Think-Pair-Share. Imagine if the teacher says "Think for a few minutes (or even seconds) about the word problem I have just put on the board. Then, turn to your learning partner and explain how you would approach this word problem. What would you do first?" Now, every student's brain is actively engaged in the task. Variations of this practice include:

- Think, Write, Pair, Share
- Think, Pair, Share, Blog
- Think, Pair, Illustrate, Share
- Think, Pair, Solve, Share
- Think, Share with a Partner, Share with a Small Group, or Share with the Class

A similar practice involves asking students to stop reading at a designated spot and "say something" to their learning partner:

- Explain why this makes sense to you—or why it doesn't.
- Make a connection from what you've read to an event in your life, to something you've heard, or to something you've read about in another text.
- Point out anything in the text (or the problem) that is confusing to you.
- Summarize the last part that you read (or worked on).

- Ask each other three questions about what you just read or saw.
- Explain how you would adapt what you just learned to something you learned earlier.
- Is there anything in the text with which you disagree? Why?
- How would you explain what you just read (or did) to a younger student?
- What more would you like to know about what you have just read?

Creating a social learning environment helps struggling students overcome negative associations with school and oppositional attitudes toward school learning itself. It is also essential for English language learners. Social interactions encourage students who are reluctant to speak out in whole-class settings to ask questions, clarify misconceptions, make connections, or perform comprehension checks in an informal, learner-friendly way.

Even if it sometimes feels as if students aren't on task or that time is being wasted, remember that the very act of students working together will have beneficial results. And if you need to justify this sometimes loud and messy approach, there is plenty of research to back you up. For example, Johnson and Johnson (1986) found that cooperative teams achieve at higher levels and retain information longer than students who work individually.

Engagement Through Self-Efficacy

Self-efficacy, the belief and determination that you can do something, is a vital component of engagement (Alvermann, 2003). Many students, such as the 10th grader who told her English teacher that she had never read a whole book in her life, believe that they simply aren't capable of reading an entire book. Fortunately, her teacher did not give up on the student. The teacher found a young adult novel by Sharon Draper, a text that was interesting to the student and *that she could read.* Indeed, the student read it from cover to cover, changing forever her perceptions about herself as a reader. Self-efficacy is so important that in a review of the research, Schunk found students who feel efficacious about learning actually achieved at higher levels (2003).

Of course, we can't change perceptions overnight. And negative perceptions are deeply ingrained, especially in those students who have been labeled as "test failers" and placed in classes for the sole purpose of turning them into "test passers"—as if their worth is determined by their ability to make a certain score on a single, standardized test. We have much work to do with these students, and it has nothing to do with filling in bubbles on a computer-scored answer sheet. Self-perception problems may be especially prevalent in math classes where students have come to believe they can't "do" math and see the numbers on the page as a blur instead of as symbols with meaning. Building students' self-efficacy can be accomplished by providing them with positive experiences that convince them that they *can* learn math, science, history, and every other subject—and they *can* read and make sense of text. What they can't do is become successful with text that is too difficult for them to read or solve problems without the necessary background knowledge. See Chapter 2 for ideas on how to build background knowledge and Chapter 4 for advice on how to help students use appropriate strategies when the text is too difficult. Chapter 7 on text sets may also help with building background knowledge.

Engagement Through Interest

Perhaps one of the most difficult components of engagement is tapping into the interests of learners. Many teachers feel they are unable to compete with the intriguing electronic gadgets that are a part of life for most of our students. We have to find a way to engage our students without turning ourselves into bone-weary slaves.

Interest is the precursor to curiosity, and, unfortunately, much of what is written in textbooks is presented without as much as a nod to curiosity. Textbook editors may turn section headings into questions or create a blurb that says "What Do You Want to Know?" but students see through such canned efforts. What does create interest, however, are the many colorful photographs, sidebars of related information, primary documents, graphs, maps, and *any* visual component that brings the textbook topic to life. These features are a form of visual literacy, and students need to learn how to read these images just as they learn to read print. Students live in a visual world and respond positively to varied arrangements of text as well as nonlinguistic features—and negatively to long sections of print unbroken by a visual interlude.

An easy way to create interest in the text is by walking students through the chapter before reading it and pointing out the visuals that beckon them on every page. Even older students sometimes skip over fascinating sidebars that can help them comprehend the content if the sidebars aren't explicitly pointed out. Nurture student interest by giving them time to talk about what they see and encourage them to ask questions or make comments. Having students make predictions about the content of the chapter based on the visuals is a good reading strategy as well as a good motivator. You may also provide "sticky notes" and ask students to write questions on them and attach the notes to visuals in their textbooks before they read. When they begin reading, students can look at the questions and see if the text provides an answer.

As the Common Core State Standards direct, we must present students with challenging text and help them learn to read long passages, but that won't happen by insisting that they read interminable pages of text, or by teaching them to answer questions by skimming the text. The ability to read for long periods of time without losing interest is a skill that comes from practice. Learning to read actively, as discussed in Chapter 4, is another way to increase prolonged reading.

Interest Through Inquiry

When students become curious about a topic, they develop interest. Often topics are presented to students simply because they are next in the textbook. In *Developing More Curious Minds,* John Barell (2003, pp. 1–19) calls on teachers to create a culture of inquisitiveness. Unfortunately, many textbooks do not engender this sort of mindset, though I did find one middle school series where the editors presented concepts in the form of case studies related to a question. I wish more of those had been included in the textbook.

When using the textbook as a resource, take one topic or concept and come at it from an inquiry stance.

- In a middle school science lesson on weather: What causes a tsunami?
- In an elementary social studies class: Why did the U.S. colonists feel so strongly about becoming independent from Britain?
- In a high school English class: Why are so many poems written about death?
- In any math class: Which operations do we need to learn and which ones can we turn over to our calculators?

In a climate of inquisitiveness, the textbook is just one more source from which we can gain information in our quest to satisfy students' curiosity. In some schools, teachers begin units by having students create essential questions. Content information is presented for the purpose of expanding or answering these questions, and students care about the information because their questions will guide their inquiry for the duration of the unit. It is all within a framework of authenticity. Textbooks, like any reference book, will meet our needs when we use them for the purpose of finding out what we need to know.

The idea of using curiosity and interest as a motivator for learning (and for decreasing the drop-out rate) is put into practice in many states that have among their graduation requirements the completion of a senior project. In Connecticut, for example, the program is specifically designed to challenge students while promoting independent study and learning (Connecticut Association of Schools, 2008, p. 1). Such a project may be a year-long or semester-long study in which a student must find an academic area of interest and engage in a research project, portfolio, internship, community service project, or other activity that may include group work, reflection, and the use of technology. The project is generally presented to a panel of evaluators, which may include community members, teachers, and professionals in the field.

With the Common Core State Standards looming, it is more important than ever to keep engagement at the forefront of complex and deep study. As Calkins, Ehrenworth, and Lehman note so elegantly, “engagement is the sine qua non for learning” (2012, p. 90).

What Engagement Isn't

One final note about engagement and textbook fatigue: Engagement doesn't mean entertainment. No one is suggesting that teachers entertain students with video games or a comedy routine that keeps them in stitches—though humor does make learning more engaging. I am not suggesting that you never introduce boring topics to students or ask them to read something about which they express little interest. On the contrary, engagement happens when you move away from the front of the room and students fill the void by actively participating in learning the content, especially once they figure out that learning for themselves is far preferable to doing “work” for their teacher.

Community of Practice: Engaging Students

In this Community of Practice, the group will conduct action research on one of Guthrie's engagement practices. See information about action research in Appendix C. Following is a suggested outline for the group's activities.

In the meeting

1. With a partner, choose one of the practices from the third column in Figure 1.1 (Classroom Practices) and discuss how you will adapt the practices to the next topic you plan to teach.

In the classroom

2. In one class, teach the lesson or unit in the traditional way you approach the lesson. In another class provide activities that focus on one or more of the practices suggested in this chapter. You may want to peruse other chapters in this book to identify activities that correlate to Guthrie's model for engagement or develop your own.
3. During the lesson, keep observational notes of the following:

- How do students initially respond to the topic in each class?
- Which class has a higher absentee rate during this "action research" period?
- Which class asked more in-depth questions during this period?
- How did assessments compare in each class?
- What informal observations can you make that will help you understand engagement?

4. Give students a survey at the end of the unit in each class that assesses their motivation and engagement in the task, such as the one in Figure 1.2.

In the follow-up meeting

5. Compare notes with others in your group and refine the activity based on your reflections.

1.2 Student Evaluation of Engagement

Student name: ______________________ Unit or topic: ______________________

Rate the following questions and feel free to add comments at the bottom of the page.

1 = Not at all 2 = Somewhat 3 = About Average 4 = More Than Average 5 = Very Much

1. When your teacher introduced this unit, how interested were you in learning about the topic?	
2. Did your engagement increase when you worked in a group or with a partner?	
3. How relevant did you find this topic to your life?	
4. Were you allowed to make choices while studying this topic (such as choosing a passage to read, a project to complete, a partner to work with)?	
5. How curious did you feel about finding out more about this topic after you got into it?	
6. To what extent will you read more about this topic or research it online after the unit is finished in class?	

Comments:

2

Background Knowledge: The Glue That Makes Learning Stick

A person's background knowledge, often called prior knowledge, is a collection of "abstracted residue" (Schallert, 2002, p. 557) that has been formed from all of life's experiences. We all, whether as a toddler or a centenarian, bring diverse bits of background knowledge—consciously or subconsciously—to every subsequent experience, and we use them to connect or glue new information to old. Background knowledge is an essential component in learning because it helps us make sense of new ideas and experiences.

Consider an early 20th century photograph shown in Figure 2.1 of a row of men with their backs to the camera, perusing information in front of a building with the sign "National Association Headquarters Opposed to Woman Suffrage." Closer to the photographer, a lone woman is also facing away from the camera, her body language indicating that she is watching and reacting to the men. If the photograph is viewed by someone who knows the term *suffrage,* he will likely understand the dramatic irony

2.1 National Anti-Suffrage Association Headquarters

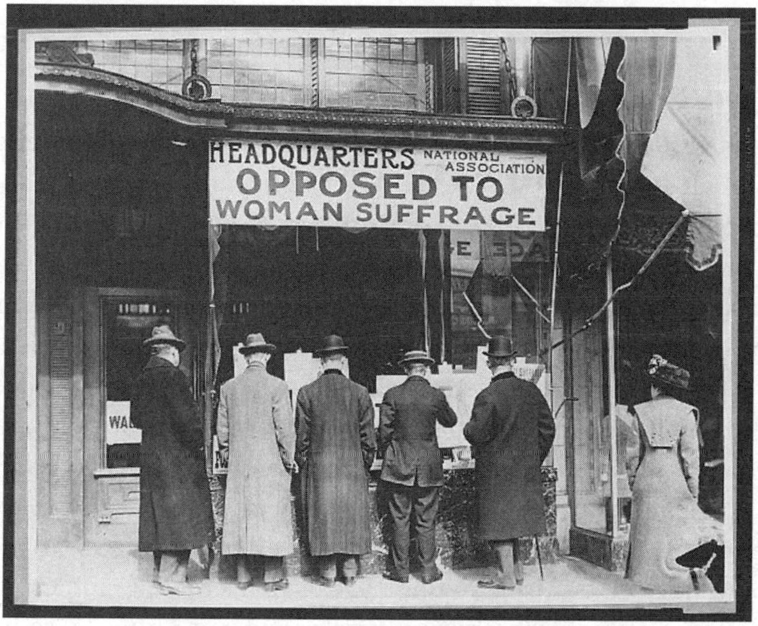

Source: Library of Congress, Prints and Photographs Division LC-USZ62-25338 DLC

portrayed in the photo. If a viewer doesn't know what suffrage means or has no background knowledge about the movement, he will be unable to "read" this piece of text. The viewer who understands the photograph is not smarter or more advanced than someone who doesn't understand it; he simply has knowledge that allows him to unlock the meaning. With a little bit of background—the definition of *suffrage,* for example—anyone may be able to answer low-level comprehension questions about the photo, but extensive prior knowledge about the suffrage movement and the violence that erupted in opposition to women's demands to vote deepens understanding of this scene. Failing to understand the photo is analogous to failing to understand print text—something that happens to students with insufficient background knowledge.

They may see the photograph—that is, pronounce words without error, read fluently, and even answer some questions about the text—but the full meaning of the text eludes them without pertinent background knowledge.

Importance of Background Knowledge

I was visiting an 8th grade social studies class soon after the tsunami hit Japan in 2011. The teacher had abandoned the textbook lesson to focus on the disaster. With copies of *USA Today* in front of them, students read about the imminent danger of the nuclear reactors having a meltdown at the Fukushima Daiichi Nuclear Power Plant. Suddenly, I realized that my background knowledge was insufficient for understanding the potential consequences. Yes, I knew that it would be a very bad thing if the nuclear reactors experienced a meltdown, but beyond that, I had no concept of a *melting* nuclear reactor. Because I cared about what happened (notice the intrinsic motivation), I read several articles about nuclear reactors online; found some simple graphics that described possible scenarios; and asked my father, a retired nuclear power plant engineer, to explain how they operate. As the gaps in my knowledge filled, my comprehension soared.

How important is background knowledge? According to Robert Marzano, "What students *already know* about the content is one of the strongest indicators of how well they will learn new information relative to the content" (2004, p. 1). John Guthrie is equally adamant as he writes about comprehension as impossible without prior knowledge (2008, p. 11), and the National Research Council states definitively, "All learning involves transfer from previous experiences. Even initial learning involves transfer that is based on previous experiences and prior knowledge" (2000, p. 236).

Background Knowledge

The problem for students and teachers, however, is obvious: the background knowledge playing field is not equal. Let's take a chapter in a science textbook on stars and planets. In a typical science classroom, especially in grades 7 and up where students may have come from a variety of elementary schools, you might have several students whose elementary science teacher worked at a planetarium during college and enthusiastically helped her students build a mock planetarium in the classroom. On the other hand, you may have a group of students whose teacher never really got into astronomy and whose background knowledge is almost nonexistent. Then there are all those other students: kids whose parents have telescopes, kids who live in brightly lit cities and never notice the night sky, and kids who search the Internet for information on constellations because they have an inherent interest in stars.

In addition, there is an affective component to prior knowledge. A good example is the knowledge 5th graders bring to a textbook chapter on the civil rights movement. Those who have visited the Kelly Ingram Civil Rights Memorial Park in Birmingham will likely have a strong visceral response when studying the bombing of the 16th Street Baptist Church in 1963, and they may have an empathetic understanding of what it feels like to be sprayed with fire hoses after viewing the displays and photographs. Students whose relatives were active in the movement may have heard so many stories that they feel like they were there, though they were not born until decades later. These students bring to the social studies or English text not only objective information but also an emotional response that creates a virtual experience as they read. Beginning with the first chapter in a textbook unit and moving lockstep through the book is not only an inefficient way to teach but is unfair both to those who have background knowledge and, more important, to those who do not.

Assessing Background Knowledge

Before beginning any chapter or unit, it is essential to find out what your students know about the topic. What students know is difficult to predict without some sort of objective measure, especially considering the ranges of background knowledge in any one class. Following are several ways to assess individuals' background knowledge and get a feel for how much the class as a whole knows about the topic.

Prediction Guides

Prediction guides, also called anticipation guides (Buehl, 2001), are one of the best ways to assess students' prior knowledge. As an added advantage, such activities give students clues about what's coming next and that helps them set a purpose for learning, an important aspect of motivation.

The idea behind a prediction guide is that the teacher provides students with written statements related to the text before they begin reading. Students indicate that they agree or disagree with these statements, and then the teacher can facilitate the discussion centered on students' reasoning for their predictions. See Figure 2.2 for a sample prediction guide on probability in 8th grade math.

Make sure that students understand that this is an activity, not a test, and that they will not be graded according to the accuracy of their answers. You can turn it into an engaging activity by inserting some crazy predictions. For example, a 4th grade science

2.2 Sample Prediction Guide on Probability

Student name: ______________________________

Read each statement and circle A if you agree with the statement or D if you disagree. Remember that this is not a test, so make your best guess.

	Agree / Disagree
1. The probability of zero means an event is impossible.	A D
2. When studying probability you may be asked to play with dice.	A D
3. The sum of the probabilities of all the possible outcomes equals one.	A D
4. Two mutually exclusive events can happen at the same time.	A D
5. You should understand fractions before beginning the study of probability.	A D

teacher gave her students a prediction guide about weather before introducing them to the chapter. One of the items asked students to agree or disagree with this statement: "Fog is really just clouds that have fallen from the sky." Some students knew that both fog and clouds are composed of water droplets, but the "falling from the sky" part made them pause and think. When asking them for their reasoning, the teacher found out who understood the concept of fogs and clouds, with a bit of fun mixed in.

Anticipation guides provide the teacher "with some understanding of the quality and quantity of prior knowledge students have about the ideas in the reading assignment" (Anders & Spitler, 2007, p. 171). When you collect the guides and tally the responses, you will see a clear pattern indicating which concepts the entire group has or has not been exposed to as well as which individuals may need additional instruction. You may return the guides to students, allowing them to change their answers as they read if they find information that contradicts what they originally believed, or you may want to have students readdress their guides at the end of the unit. An added benefit is that once students invest in a prediction, they are eager to find out if they are right, and the information often sticks with them longer because of that investment.

In any case, you will have a much better idea about how to approach the chapter or unit after you take a look at your students' responses. Design your instruction to specifically meet students' needs. You may put less knowledgeable students in a group with a student tutor who has more knowledge; you may jigsaw the reading so that students who already know a little about the topic read a different part of the text and share what they learned with other students; or you may offer extended learning opportunities, including online research, to those who have solid background knowledge.

Although creating prediction guides can take time, one easy way to accumulate several for every topic is to have students write their own prediction guides when they finish the unit. The exercise serves as a great review for your students prior to assessment and gives you a variety of prediction guides by the end of the year. You can choose among the best statements for next year's (or next semester's) students. Not surprisingly, you will find that students' statements are often more creative than those we write. Use the following tips to assist students in writing their own guides:

1. Skim the chapter and find the most important ideas related to the topic. Write a few statements about each. Aim for 10 statements per guide.
2. Use short and succinct sentences, avoiding absolute words such as never, always, best, or worst.
3. Play around by including funny or crazy predictions to make the activity enjoyable.
4. Avoid vocabulary that is too difficult or specific.
5. Explore your questions and thoughts and don't worry about following the chapter exactly.

Carousel Walk

A carousel walk (or gallery walk) allows students to work in groups and move around the room as they share background knowledge. Suppose your next unit in your middle or high school social studies or English curriculum is the story of Homer's Ulysses (or Odysseus). Although you may simply ask who has read the story, seen a movie about the adventure, or heard the tale, you won't know if students have misinformation or superficial knowledge without a more in-depth assessment. Begin by listing various aspects of the story that you think are important. If you have taught the story before, you already know what you want students to learn. If you haven't, look through the unit in the textbook and note important concepts designated by headings or illustrations. Now the fun begins.

1. Write one word or term on a separate sheet of chart paper. Examples may include Trojan horse, Penelope, Cyclops, Circe, Sirens, Ulysses, Ithaca, or even concepts such as bravery,

adventure, or journey. Tape charts around the room on walls, allowing about five feet between charts.

2. Place students in groups of three or four and give each group leader a different colored marker.

3. Station one group by each chart. When you say "begin," the students in each group will list everything they know about the term. When you say "move," they will advance to the chart on their right and begin listing everything they know about that term until you again say "move." Groups move and add to the lists until they return to their original charts.

4. Have students sit down (within their groups) and go through each chart with the whole class, reading the items aloud and asking for clarification from the groups (easily identifiable by the color of the marker used). You can foster discussions and make connections as you assess, activate, and build background knowledge prior to reading.

Free Discussion

One of my favorite ways of assessing background knowledge is by listening to kids talk. I put students in groups (or allow them to choose groups) and throw out a question related to the reading, such as "Why do you feel lighter in water than out of it?" when studying buoyancy in elementary science or "What do you know about China?" before beginning a unit on China in social studies, any grade. Each group shares what they know (or think they know) while I listen carefully. Students often say things that are far from fact, so this activity gives me opportunities to correct misperceptions or ask them to look up information online and then report back to the class the next day.

Building Background Knowledge

Once you have gained insights about what your students know, you can create lessons that target specific learning, something textbooks simply cannot do. It takes a teacher who knows his students to differentiate, and the more you assess background knowledge and teach to your students' strengths, the better you will become at focusing your instruction.

Many textbooks try to help you by offering a section called Activating Background Knowledge or something similar, but such a cursory approach to activating prior knowledge is not enough. In our earlier example about stars, for instance, one middle-school textbook directs the teacher to build background by asking students if they have ever observed the Milky Way in the night sky. Such questions may guide students toward the topic, but they are hardly sufficient for building or accessing prior knowledge. Even if students' backgrounds were activated through such a question, it doesn't mean that they will automatically connect what they know to what they are learning. You know how easily students can take a question meant to build background and turn it into a narrative that is tangential to what you are trying to teach: "Oh, yeah, I have seen the Milky Way. One time my Uncle Frank took us out to a field in the middle of the night and we had hot chocolate and . . . ." It is important to explicitly help students connect what they know about a topic to what you want them to learn about it.

As I noted in Chapter 1, an engaging way to connect what students know to what they are learning is to take advantage of the visuals offered in textbooks and do a walk-through with your students, prompting them to speak out if they know something about a graphic or text feature. A 6th grade science textbook includes a shocking photograph of a house that slid down a hill during heavy rains. The written text, unfortunately, is little more than fact after fact about El Niño and La Niña with a reference to landslides and erosion but no explanation of either word. It wouldn't take much time to have students look carefully at the photograph, explain to them how such an event happens, and ask them to look up landslides or mudslides online, perhaps finding other photographs to share. Then when students read in their textbooks "During an El Niño period, warmer surface water in areas of the eastern equatorial Pacific Ocean leads to more water vapor being in the air above the water. This can result in increased rainfall across the southeastern United States" (McGraw-Hill/Glencoe, 2007, p. 479), they may have enough background knowledge to stick with the text and even comprehend the effects of El Niño.

Textbook Scavenger Hunts

In some schools or districts, teachers are still required to use textbooks for every lesson. Teachers who have few supplemental text choices often feel frustrated by their lack of options in dealing with the textbook. This activity makes the most of what textbooks have to offer and builds background in the process. Create a textbook scavenger hunt for important ideas, visuals, or new vocabulary before asking students to read the chapter. In groups of two or three, have students go on a virtual scavenger hunt (within the textbook) using a list of items that you have created to build background knowledge. Groups will then share what they have discovered with everyone in the class. You may want to assign one or two items to each group and facilitate a jigsawing of information. This active, enjoyable method of building background will add to students' understanding of the text when they begin reading. Here are sample items for your textbook chapter scavenger hunt:

- Choose five words or terms the group thinks will be important to this unit. (Note: Don't use the vocabulary words that are highlighted at the beginning of the chapter.)
- Choose one picture in this chapter and tell why your group thinks this picture is important.
- Choose one graph or map and provide a different caption for it.
- Give a summary of the cycle on page *X*.
- Write the items needed for the lab on page *X*. Think of two more items that would be useful for this experiment.
- Find the answer to one "review" math problem in this chapter.
- Record something in this chapter that your group has studied in previous years and discuss what new information is presented.

• List three things to look up online that would help your group better understand this chapter.

• Discuss which visual in this chapter is most interesting to your group. Explain why.

• Discuss which concept in this chapter your group thinks may be most difficult to understand.

Using Picture Books to Build Background

Picture books, sometimes known as children's books, aren't just for little kids anymore. Surprisingly, picture books contain more rare words per thousand words than prime-time television or the conversation of college graduates (Carr, Buchannan, Wentz, Weiss, & Brant, 2001). A quick perusal of what are called crossover picture books, nonfiction and fiction books for adolescent and adult readers with complex themes and provocative subject matter, will convince you that this new category of books is certainly not written for kindergarteners. They are, however, excellent resources for building background because they focus on a single concept, often in depth.

The authors of *The Power of Picture Books: Using Content-Area Literature in Middle School* note, "Academically, picture book topics offer valuable extensions to subject area content and, in many cases, go far beyond the basic information in the textbook" (Fresch & Harkins, 2009, p. 6). When teaching probability in math, as we discussed earlier, the authors talk about a math teacher who used a picture book, *A Very Improbable Story* (Einhorn, 2008), to help his students understand real-life application. Picture books build background through visual images as well as through words, an especially important factor for this generation of visual learners. Powerful and poignant images found in picture books trigger memories or make connections in meaningful ways.

As for building background, the illustrations and text come together in a way that textbooks simply cannot by giving students a rich context prior to reading. For example, Maya Angelou's poem paired with graffiti artist Jean-Michel Basquiat's illustrations in the picture book *Life Doesn't Frighten Me* (1993) creates an experience that deepens meaning for middle or high school English students preparing to read Angelou's *I Know Why the Caged Bird Sings* (1983).

In social studies, the picture book *Patrol: An American Soldier in Vietnam* by Walter Dean Myers (2005) is another example of this phenomenon. The young soldier in this picture book expresses his fear of dying and tries to understand who the enemy is. "In war, shadows are enemies, too," he thinks (p. 7). In this powerful story-poem, Myers takes us into the war as we share this soldier's unforgettable experience. The illustrations by Ann Grifalconi look like cut-outs glued together to make a collage, and along with the infusion of camouflage, they add another dimension to the reading experience.

Picture books for science and English topics abound as well, from books about Gregor Mendel (Bardoe, 2006) to books that introduce readers to the poetry of William Carlos Williams (Bryant, 2008). There are even picture books for math teachers, the most famous being the *Sir Cumference* series by Cindy Neuschwander for elementary students. *Pythagoras and the Ratios: A Math Adventure* (Ellis, 2010) is a good picture book for older students.

Be on the lookout, as well, for longer nonfiction books on a variety of topics: *Flesh and Blood so Cheap: The Triangle Fire and Its Legacy* (Marrin, 2011), *Journey into the Deep: Discovering New Ocean Creatures* (Johnson, 2010), *Claudette Colvin: Twice Toward Justice* (Hoose, 2010), or *We've Got a Job: The 1963 Birmingham Children's March* (Levinson, 2012). You won't be able to read these books to students in one sitting, but you could read a chapter a day or make them available to students who need extra help with background on particular topics. Many of these books have won prestigious awards, so don't hesitate to ask your media specialist to order them to place on the library or reading shelf. You may also want to check out the Orbis Pictus Awards for outstanding nonfiction picture books at http://www.ncte.org/awards/orbispictus.

Building Background Virtually

In classrooms equipped with interactive whiteboards—or if all students have laptops or tablets—building background knowledge is easier than ever before. Websites allow students virtual experiences, such as listening to speeches or music from different eras; watching video clips or newscasts; or examining all sorts of primary documents. These background builders significantly deepen students' comprehension of any topic.

The best part of technology is that you can get students to help you. Look through the chapter or unit you are preparing to teach. After assessing students' background knowledge, decide what topics you will scaffold with additional information. In a middle school social studies book, for example, a chapter on India offers a picture of Mohandas Karamchand (Mahatma) Gandhi, but only one sentence about him. If you want to teach students about India by focusing on Gandhi, perhaps in conjunction with the English teacher's unit on biographies, have students go to http://www.mkgandhi.org/main.htm, a wide-ranging site about Gandhi that contains primary documents, student projects from other countries, speeches, video clips, and more. You can assign different groups topics to research or ask individual students to look on the site and be prepared to discuss something they learned about Gandhi with their groups.

Current textbooks may also be helpful because they often include lists of websites or DVDs of supplemental material such as film clips, music, or photographs. Digital textbooks have links that will take students all over the world instantly. The hard part is deciding which topics need to be expanded through background information. In the short textbook chapter on India, I found more than 30 different topics, from monsoons to reincarnation. Clearly, you cannot build background knowledge on each of those topics. The obvious advantage is found in exploring one topic in depth, such as Gandhi, and building a comprehensive understanding of India through his life, rather than having students read one unrelated sentence after another about some place in the world called India.

Building Background Through Experiences

Robert Marzano discusses the importance of direct experiences: "The most straightforward way to enhance students' academic background knowledge is to provide academically enriching experiences." He defines the direct approach as one that increases "the variety and depth of out-of-class experiences. Such experiences include field trips to museums, art galleries, and the like, as well as school-sponsored travel and exchange programs" (2004, p. 14).

Hands-on or direct experiences help students understand concepts they encounter while reading and support other activities such as writing or discussions. Many schools and districts assert that money does not exist for such activities, but money may be found through grants, parent-teacher associations, parent contributions, or even candy sales. If it is impossible to take students out of the school setting, then bring the world to students. Often parents, community, and faculty members have vast resources in terms of experiences and artifacts. Let parents and faculty know the topics you will be covering and ask if anyone would be willing to help you create experiences for the students. I will never forget the year that my team-teacher and I were teaching a unit on the Vietnam antiwar movement when we discovered that a student's parent attended Kent State and had witnessed the shootings in 1970. She came to our class and talked about what she had seen, and we were all mesmerized by her account. Hearing her firsthand story brought the experience into our lives in a personal, memorable way.

Similarly, my students often told me that seeing plays by a variety of playwrights at the Shakespeare Festival, going to art museums to experience visual literacy, interviewing residents at a retirement home, and participating in other experiences that I created related to our study were significant factors in their education. I remember one autumn day when we were reading *Of Mice and Men* (Steinbeck, 2002), and I led my high school students outside so they could walk across the fallen leaves and listen to how they crunched under their feet in just the way

Steinbeck described. A minimal attempt at building background knowledge, you may think, but I contend that such experiences *do* enhance students' understanding and motivate them to make those important connections each time they read a text.

Next Best: Virtual Field Trips

A virtual tour on a website pales in comparison to any field trip, especially an active one such as to a space center. If you've ever talked to a kid who took a field trip to a space center, you know what I mean. Many students have decided to pursue a career in science or engineering because of their experience at one of these centers. They vividly remember talking with astronauts, placing their hands on a space shuttle, or experiencing a simulation of a lift-off. Although the pictures and online tours are better than nothing, they come in a distant second to the real deal.

I recommend a direct experience over a virtual field trip, but we all know that real field trips are often impossible. The next best thing is a virtual field trip; many online sites work hand-in-hand with educators. Middle school teacher Dan Jones told his local newspaper, "I can take them (students) on location to Egypt and they can do a presentation in front of the Great Pyramid of Giza." (*Mansfield News Journal,* 2011). Jones uses technology made by a company called Yoostar, which allows his students to appear in real time on a computer screen as if they are on location. He also used Skype to connect 8th graders to Ford's Theater when they were studying Abraham Lincoln.

Go to http://www.simplek12.com/virtualfieldtrips and download virtual trips for history, social studies, fine arts, English, math, science, and many other subjects. Many of these tours have been put together by students or teachers and are educationally sound. Another site that offers a wide variety of experiences is http://www.internet4classrooms.com, where you'll find links for Internet sites specifically for K–8 students. At http://www.theteachersguide.com/virtualtours.html you'll find virtual tours of all sorts of museums, including the National

Gallery of Art (Washington, DC) and the U.S. Holocaust Memorial Museum, as well as of historical sites including the Great Wall of China and Gettysburg National Battlefield Park (Pennsylvania). I could list hundreds of websites offering virtual field trips, but you'll do better by simply using a search engine to explore your topic and choosing a website that will fill in the gaps in your students' background knowledge. Better yet, teach students how to be skeptical consumers of online information and allow them to engage in their own personal, albeit virtual, field trips.

Reading as a Background Builder

As I have mentioned, one of the most significant problems with textbooks is that they tend to narrow the curriculum to what will be tested, often resulting in a brief overview of many subjects. The overview can leave students both overwhelmed with lists, facts, and dry recitations of topics and underprepared for attaching new learning to old.

Kelly Gallagher in *Readicide* (2009) argues that the focus on testing preparation robs students of the opportunity to build background through wide and varied reading. This is painfully and ironically true, but what can you do about it? Gallagher suggests that teachers provide students with an article a week in an effort to build prior knowledge for learning *and* for doing well on tests. "Those students who sit down to the exam with the broadest base of prior knowledge will have the highest chance of scoring well" (2009, p. 38). He provides a list of the articles of the week that he has used at www.kellygallagher.org/resources/articles.htm.

I recommend that teachers go further in making sure that students have a consistent and wide range of reading experiences by creating a literacy-rich environment in each content-area class. Calkins, Ehrenworth, and Lehman (2012) put this issue in perspective.

> One textbook often costs thirty thousand dollars for classroom sets. And often these texts can't begin to match the

> complexity of good primary and secondary sources. If you are aligning instruction to the Common Core, you will need students to read well-crafted texts that are written with particular (and different) perspectives. This suggests that your school will need to *channel whatever resources you do have away from textbooks and toward trade books.* (p. 93)

Following are some suggestions about how to make that happen.

Create student text detectives. Ask students to find news articles or information related to current events or the topic you are teaching every week or so. Allow students to sign up for a particular day in advance and have them bring in an article to share with the class. Students could also choose a visual, a cartoon, or an online news clip instead of a printed newspaper article. You may require that students show you the piece a few days before it is presented to check for validity. Text detectives is a quick activity but loaded with new learning. It should take no more than 10 minutes of class time for students to present their news. An added benefit is that students will expand their reading and their background knowledge by looking for articles to present on their assigned day.

Create a large classroom library. Collect a broad selection of young adult novels and nonfiction titles related to your discipline. Although this is a common practice for English and social studies teachers, math and science teachers can include biographies of mathematicians or scientists as well as books on discoveries. A trend in young adult literature is forensic novels. Go to http://www.teenreads.com or have students look through the site to find books that will build background knowledge and get them reading like crazy. Assign a class librarian to keep track of checked out books and make sure students have both time and motivation for choosing and reading books. If you don't have a class library, ask your media specialist to pull a group of books related to the topic of study that you can return at the end of the unit. See Chapter 7 for more information about text sets and lists to help you build a classroom library.

Provide primary documents for every topic you introduce. The Library of Congress at http://myloc.gov offers diaries, photographs, songs, journals, and news articles from hundreds of time periods related to thousands of topics. Again, ask students to take on the responsibility of finding relevant documents so you don't have to do all the work. Students can also be in charge of creating bulletin boards to display these pieces as they build background knowledge.

Get a classroom set of current events materials. Talk to your reading coach or media specialist about subscribing to a class set of current events magazines, either print or online. Magazines targeted for the reading level of your students, such as *Time for Kids* for younger students or *New York Times Upfront* for older students, contain the latest news in all disciplines.

In one school, the reading coach sent a copy of the table of contents of each weekly current events magazine to every teacher. With that simple prompt, teachers could request the entire set of magazines or have students access the online version so they could read articles relevant to the topics they were studying. Being aware of the topics in the magazines gave teachers natural segues into opportunities for building interdisciplinary background experiences. In a middle school, an interdisciplinary team of English, social studies, science, and math teachers used the account of the Chilean miners who were trapped 2,300 feet below Earth's surface to cover their standards in an engaging way that was relevant to students—while building background in all of those disciplines.

Even the covers of these newsmagazines are valuable in building background. If allowed, students can create a timeline of events that happened during the year by hanging the covers on the wall in sequence or by clipping them to a high kite string hung across the room.

Background Knowledge: A Necessity

Background knowledge is not a frill of education, a nicety that simply helps students enjoy reading and learning. Background knowledge is essential to comprehension, to making connections, and to understanding the big ideas. Background knowledge is the foundation of all academic study. Not taking the time to assess, activate, and build prior knowledge is like throwing the ball to an inexperienced basketball player and demanding that he play like a pro in the big game.

All learning takes time, and it is incremental. No matter how quickly the textbook skips from topic to topic, it is our responsibility to help students fill in the blanks so meaning is complete and rewarding.

Community of Practice: Building Background

For this Community of Practice, the group will engage in designing activities that will help students build background knowledge.

In the meeting

1. In content-area groups or with a colleague, make a list of topics that you feel are most important to cover this term or semester. Spend time discussing what is really important and resist the urge to list every topic that might possibly be on a test.

2. At subsequent meetings, examine a topic before you start to teach it. Brainstorm how you can build background knowledge:

- What direct experiences could you provide to build students' background?
- What virtual experiences could you provide students using various media, including the Internet, music, and primary documents?
- What supplemental reading or research (for all ability levels) would build background pertinent to this topic?
- Whom could you invite to talk to groups of students about relevant topics?
  - Faculty or staff member with firsthand experience or knowledge?
  - Community member, group, or parent with experience or knowledge about a topic?
  - Professional from a local business in a related discipline?

In the classroom

3. Use the materials and information from the brainstorming session to share background knowledge with your students. Collect information from the classroom experience to help members reflect after the lesson and at your next group meeting. Ask your students to evaluate how building background affected their learning.

4. If possible, compare the assessment scores of groups of students with whom you built background with those who did not have that advantage, perhaps using scores from last year's students.

In the follow-up meeting

5. Give an example of how you helped students build background knowledge; offer your evaluation of the activity, including feedback from students and an analysis based on a group of students that did not benefit from background knowledge; share data with each other.

3

Vocabulary IS the Content

I don't know what it was like when you were in school, but I remember vocabulary study as one of the most boring parts of the day. It went something like this: I tackled my lists of words by looking them up in fat blue dictionaries, never quite remembering if *L* comes before or after *K*, so words beginning with those letters were especially troublesome. Then, I copied definitions that sometimes made no sense to me, all numbered as if they weren't related. Finally, I used the words in sentences, something I liked to do if I could figure out what the word *really* meant.

As opposed to vocabulary *study,* words used in context fascinated me. I have a memory of reading Rip Van Winkle, maybe in the 7th grade, and learning the word *incessant,* which I thought was a cool word—just say it and you'll see what I mean. Rip's wife talked incessantly, as I recall, and I liked that too; it made sense to me because I had a neighbor who also talked incessantly. I could picture Rip's wife rattling on while he daydreamed about his outings. *Incessant* stayed with me, became a part of my permanent vocabulary bank, and I still like using it today.

Who Chooses Vocabulary Words?

If you look at an English textbook with the story of Rip Van Winkle, the inevitable vocabulary list introduces the story. Some of the words are archaic, others are current, but the list is usually long. Most textbooks use footnotes or sidebars so that students can easily find the meanings of difficult words while reading. If they are fortunate enough to be reading the story in a digital textbook, students can find the meaning of the word instantly and apply the definition to the context—a real advantage. No matter the format, you only have so long to spend on this story, and teaching vocabulary as presented in the textbook, could take several days. The vocabulary problem is exacerbated in content-area texts such as math, science, or social studies where vocabulary is absolutely essential for comprehension. When studying topographic maps in 6th grade social studies, for example, students must have a common understanding of *elevation, contour lines,* and *relief* to even begin to comprehend the concept.

Relying on the words chosen by the textbook editors has several inherent problems. Most obviously, the editors don't know your students, their abilities, background, or the environment in which they are living. Some students may know words from a previous class or personal experience, but others may have no knowledge of the topic. It is up to you to make informed decisions about what vocabulary your students should learn, what meanings you should provide for them while reading, and what vocabulary you can reasonably expect that they already know. Then, you must decide how to best teach the vocabulary, even when the editors have given you a variety, perhaps too much of a variety, of activities from which to choose.

Vocabulary is equally important for comprehending *all* texts that your students read, including websites and online articles, as well as fiction and nonfiction books. Students who don't understand key vocabulary can't possibly comprehend the ideas behind a particular topic, chapter, or unit of study. Learning new vocabulary is really the same as learning new content, and asking a student to read a text without providing sufficient vocabulary study is like unlocking a door in the dark.

What IS Good Vocabulary Study?

The research on vocabulary study is clear and makes perfect sense to anyone who has ever had a hobby or specialized interest. As an example, say this series of words to students who like cars and they will know immediately that you are talking car racing: *safety barrier, g-force, kill switch, anti-spill bladder, HANS, Sprint Cup, FIA Formula One, COT (Car of Tomorrow)*. For some of us, to comprehend an article about car racing means that we'd have to ask someone else a lot of questions, mostly related to vocabulary. So, it's no surprise that the main finding regarding vocabulary is that vocabulary knowledge is fundamental to reading comprehension. One simply cannot understand content without knowing what most of the words mean (Nagy, 1988). But that's only the tip of the proverbial iceberg because there are different ways of knowing words.

Let's take one of these racing terms, *FIA Formula One,* in our scenario. When I look up the definition online, I find that *Formula One,* also known as *Formula 1* or *F1,* is officially referred to as the *FIA Formula One World Championship,* the highest class of single-seater auto racing sanctioned by the Fédération Internationale de l'Automobile (FIA). *Formula* in the name refers to a set of rules to which all participants' cars must comply.

After looking up the definitions, I could certainly pass a multiple-choice test on these racing terms or do a matching exercise (which is the primary way textbooks assess students on vocabulary knowledge), so you may say that I have a working knowledge of the words. If I score an *A* on my vocabulary test, you might even go so far as to say that I am proficient with the terms. But the problem is that I don't have a conceptualized understanding of this vocabulary. Returning to the term *FIA Formula One,*

3.1 Formula 1 Race Car

Source: [©Thinkstock]/[iStockphoto]/Thinkstock.

I could continue reading that the F1 season consists of a series of races, held on purposefully built circuits and public roads. Without understanding that F1 cars can race at speeds up to 220 mph, however, and that Formula One is *the* huge television event for these race fans, I might still be in the dark. Actually, it would be best if I could attend a race or watch one on TV to build my background knowledge. Since that probably won't happen, I should at least look at a photograph of a Formula One car—a car similar to the one in Figure 3.1—because, again, if I search online for a definition and find this one on Wikipedia, I am still pretty confused: A single-seat, open cockpit, open-wheel race car with substantial front and rear wings and an engine positioned behind the driver (accessed 2/16/12). If I were to draw it, I would create some sort of angel with an engine. I simply don't have enough information to fully comprehend the description, which, by the way, is why visual literacy is so important and why it is essential to spend time showing students the graphics and photographs in textbooks. Finding a nonlinguistic representation of a vocabulary term, perhaps finding a photo of a Formula 1 race car online, would give me a better understanding of the term.

Tiering Words

We've determined that Formula 1 may be an important term for me to understand if I want to decipher a text on racing, and the term is easily footnoted. What about the others? Here's where my teacher would need to make some decisions. He might decide that *anti-spill bladder* isn't an essential word for me to know, but that I need a quick definition of *kill switch* to understand safety. He might also determine that he needs to help me understand *g-force, safety barrier,* and *HANS* for complete comprehension.

Sorting the words into groups by determining their difficulty or familiarity is described by Beck, McKeown, and Kucan as tiering words. Tier one words are generally familiar to your students and rarely require instruction—unless your students don't know the meanings of these words. The second tier contains words that are of "high frequency for mature language users and are found across a variety of domains" (2002, p. 8). Second-tier words require explicit instruction because they are important for comprehending the content. The third tier is made up of words that students may encounter only infrequently, and are perhaps related to a specific subject area. These words are ones that you might briefly explain and then move on.

Marzano points out that students' conceptual understandings increase dramatically when they are familiar with academic vocabulary before reading (2004, p. 110). Your thoughtful analysis of vocabulary words, before you have students read the textbook or any source of information in your subject area, is critical to helping students understand the content. You could begin by dividing the vocabulary words listed in your textbook into tiers.

As an example, before beginning a unit on erosion, pull relevant vocabulary words from an 8th grade science textbook and separate them into tiers or categories. See Figure 3.2 for an example. The categories will look different based on your students' grade levels, prior knowledge, and your specific teaching objectives.

After you have categorized the vocabulary list for the unit, have students write tier one and tier two words in the first column of a form similar to Figure 3.3. Then, students simply check the column that corresponds to their knowledge of the word and turn it in for your analysis (not a grade). The information you gain from this simple survey provides the data that you need to plan

3.2 Sample Word Differentiation Chart

Tier 1 Words	Tier 2 Words	Tier 3 Words
Precipitation Vegetation Gully Gravity Landslide	Sedimentation Weathering Deforestation Scouring Slumping Mass wasting Hydraulic action	Terminal velocity Isostatic depression Avulsion Accretion Littoral drift

good vocabulary instruction. The survey is an important tool because it shifts responsibility for learning directly back to the student even before the lesson begins.

You might be surprised to find that some students don't know the words you put in tier 1, in which case you can plan small group instruction or pair students to work together. Conversely,

3.3 Word Familiarity Chart

Name: ______________________________

List the vocabulary words in column 1 and mark the column that best corresponds to your knowledge of the word.

Vocabulary Word	Know it. Can use it in a sentence.	Might know it. Might be able to guess at its meaning.	Have heard it. Could not use it in a sentence or define it.	Never heard it. Have no idea what it means.

Source: From *Literacy for Real. Reading, Thinking, and Learning in the Content Areas*, by ReLeah Cossett Lent, 2009, New York: Teachers College Press. Copyright Teachers College Press. Adopted by permission.

there may be words (tier 2 or above) that you didn't expect students to know but that they do know, in which case you can offer a quick review or skip instruction on those words completely. Tailoring the vocabulary lesson to each student's needs makes much more sense than assigning a generic list of words to all classes and students.

Vocabulary Study in Textbooks

Textbook publishers are paying attention to vocabulary study because they understand the importance of vocabulary in accessing content. Print textbooks often highlight words in yellow, offer definitions in the margins, show students that words are used in different ways, or use vocabulary in illustrations. They also provide many examples and give explanations that begin "In other words" or "Some examples include" to help illuminate meanings. Digital textbooks, as I noted earlier, offer dictionary definitions at the touch of a key (or word) and have other features that help students understand words in context. Despite all advantages, the "cover it all" approach most textbooks take is a detriment to deep vocabulary study. Many textbooks use too many new words too quickly, without adequate explanation. I found these words on a two-page spread in a high school biology textbook:

coccus	binary fission	photosynthetic organisms
gram stain	anaerobic bacteria	mycobacterium tuberculosis
pilus	obligate aerobes	syphilis
cellular respiration	Treponema pallidum	endospores
obligate anaerobes	fermentation	sterilize
botulism	germinate	
cytoplasm	spirillum	
bacillus	conjugation	

Many of the words were defined briefly, such as "Mycobacterium tuberculosis, the organism that causes the lung disease called tuberculosis, is an obligate aerobe" (Glencoe, 2004, p. 491). The sheer number of words suggests too much vocabulary thrown at readers too quickly, and that pace exists in lower level textbooks as well. A 4th grade science textbook highlighted *adaptation* as one of many vocabulary words to be learned in the unit. It was defined in a paragraph as "a body part or a behavior that a living thing gets from its parents and that helps it survive" (Harcourt School Publishers, 2009, p. 362). Although several examples are given after that definition, the word *adaptation* is not repeated and no connection is made between the examples and the word. The teacher certainly has her work cut out for her. Not only must she choose the most important words to teach, but she must provide conceptual meanings for the words students need to know.

Model of Good Textbook Vocabulary Use

If your textbook offers definitions that *you* have to read twice because they are so complex or if it does not offer examples or explanations for words that you expect might be new or difficult for your students, I suggest changing textbooks if possible or working mostly with supplemental resources. Ideally, textbooks should approach vocabulary by presenting the words in the following way:

- Previewing a word and connecting it to students' background,
- Defining the word in a student-friendly way,
- Giving an example of how the word is used, and
- Using it in various ways several more times in the chapter.

Let's look at the term *weathering*, which often appears in a 6th grade science textbook because it is an important concept in a unit on erosion. The following paragraph is an example of how text could be written to give students a complete understanding of this word.

> You may think *weather* just has to do with temperatures, storms, and wind, but it has another meaning as well. In science, *weathering* is a process that breaks down and changes rocks at the Earth's surface. You can see where weathering comes from when you understand that rocks

deteriorate because *weather* elements such as water, wind, and ice break down larger rocks into smaller and smaller pieces. There are two types of weathering that we'll look at later on in this chapter, physical and chemical weathering, but for now let's make sure we understand the basic term *weathering*. Look at the pictures of the Sphinx on this page. The one on the left is how it probably looked when it was created and the one on the right is what it looks like now because of weathering. Turn to your partner and talk about what type of weathering you think might have happened to change the limestone face of the Sphinx.

If your textbook does not deal with vocabulary clearly, show students how you would rewrite a paragraph to help them better comprehend the words. Then have them work with a partner and rewrite a different paragraph in a similar way. You may also want students to leave sticky notes on the pages in the textbooks with key paragraphs rewritten in a way that fully explains important words for the next group of students. If your students are using digital textbooks, they may also be written in a manner that is difficult to understand; unfortunately, instant access to definitions doesn't necessarily create deep understanding.

Effective Practices for Teaching Vocabulary

Lots of books, articles, and research are related to vocabulary, but one of the most succinct studies I have found comes from an article titled "Guidelines for Evaluating Vocabulary Instruction." The authors provide the following realistic suggestions for vocabulary study.

- Instruction should help students relate new vocabulary to their background knowledge.
- Instruction should help students develop elaborated word knowledge.
- Instruction should provide for active student involvement in learning new vocabulary.

- Instruction should develop students' strategies for acquiring new vocabulary independently. (Carr & Wixson, 1986, p. 588)

Relate New Vocabulary to Background Knowledge

As we discussed in Chapter 2, background information is a powerful indicator of how well students learn new information related to content. Similarly, when students can tap into background knowledge related to vocabulary words, they are able to understand the words more readily and comprehend text more easily. You will find many activities for helping students develop or activate background knowledge in Chapter 2, and some of those same approaches may also be useful for vocabulary study. Following are two examples from the many vocabulary activities available that can help students make bridges from their knowledge to the new words. The key is in choosing the best instructional practice for your particular students and topic. You may need to try out a few activities to find the one that works best for a particular unit, since not all strategies or instructional practices work equally well for all topics or audiences.

Vocabulary mix up. A good prereading activity helps students become actively involved in word learning as well as building background knowledge. Vocabulary mix up is also effective as a review of terms after reading. Use it for introducing major topics that rely on specific vocabulary associated with the concept, such as *planes* in math, *circulatory system* in science, *nationalism* in social studies, or for vocabulary related to a short story or poem in English.

Place one vocabulary word on a table tent. For example, if you are teaching plant cells in elementary grades science, you might make six table tents, with one word on each tent: *cell membrane, cell wall, vacuole, cytoplasm, nucleus,* and *plastid.* Provide textbooks and other source material, chart paper, and markers at each table. Assign students to a table and give them roles, such as reader, illustrator, leader, and reporter. Have each group draw, define, and explain the term using available resources.

When everyone is finished, each group's reporter shares the chart with the rest of the class. Hang the charts on the wall for an enlarged word wall. A word wall works for any topic that has specific vocabulary, such as the Boston Tea Party in 5th grade social studies: *Tea Act, Townshend Act, Boston Harbor, East India Company, boycott, parliament.*

Questioning Cards. This activity is useful for deepening word meanings while building background. Tell students the meaning of a word using simple language. Give students an index card and have them write the word on a card. Direct the students to use the back of the card to respond to a prompt such as the following:

- In social studies: "If you and your friends were part of a modern *nomadic* tribe, what would your lives be like?"
- In earth science: "If you had the strength of Superman and were stuck between two shifting *tectonic plates,* what would you do?"
- In math: "If you were a *variable* in math, what would your role be?"
- In English: "If you were faced with the type of *discrimination* the main character experienced, how would you respond?"

Have students share their answers with their learning partners. Using questioning cards provides students with multiple exposures to a word, one of the guidelines for vocabulary instruction that Michael Graves advocates in *The Vocabulary Book* (2005). Researchers and teachers agree that the key for building background for vocabulary is to use words repeatedly and in various ways *before* giving students text to read or a task to perform. By laying a solid foundation, students' chances of internalizing concepts vastly improve.

Develop Elaborated Word Knowledge

When we think about almost any word, especially one with complex or multiple meanings, we see how many ways there are of knowing a word. There are superficial meanings, context-bound definitions, connotative understandings, and even tags for meaning. The more associations we have with words and the more we understand the relationship among words, the better our comprehension when we read texts that use the word. It follows that the more students see, hear, and appropriately use words, the deeper their understanding not only of that word but of the entire topic related to the word. Such elaborated word study is the best way to help students increase their vocabulary skills. You can help students deepen their word knowledge using the following activities.

Model for Elaborating Word Knowledge. Marzano and Pickering offer a 6-step process for teaching new terms that help students elaborate meanings of words.

> 1. Provide a description, explanation, or example of the new term.
> 2. Ask students to restate the description, explanation, or example in their own words.
> 3. Ask students to construct a picture, symbol, or graphic representing the term.
> 4. Engage students periodically in activities that help them add to their knowledge of the terms in their notebooks.
> 5. Periodically ask students to discuss the terms with one another.
> 6. Involve students in games that allow them to play with terms. (2005, pp. 14–15)

Suppose you decide to use this framework to explain metamorphic rocks in 3rd or 8th grade science. Your instruction might look like the following.

1. Show students a photograph of a metamorphic rock from the textbook or other source and explain how the rock was formed from heat and pressure.
2. Ask students to use their own words to restate the description in the vocabulary section of their learning log.

3. Ask small groups of students to draw a picture of a metamorphic rock, find examples of metamorphic rocks online, or create a graphic that in some way explains the process of how metamorphic rocks are created.

4. Ask students to reserve a space under the term in their logs for recording other information about the word as the unit progresses, such as types of metamorphism.

5. Display rocks, show them to pairs of students, and have them explain to each other why they are or are not metamorphic rocks.

Express Meanings in Various Ways. I advocate learning logs for each subject. Basically, logs are places where students become independent learners by differentiating what and how they learn (see Chapter 5 for more information). Vocabulary learning logs offer students an easy means of differentiating or elaborating their learning. For example, one student may have a good understanding of the Cuban Missile Crisis because her grandfather is from Cuba and has told her about it. Her social studies vocabulary log related to this topic might have more complete meanings than a student who is first introduced to the term.

In the vocabulary section of their learning logs, students keep track of their new vocabulary words, both from the textbook and from other sources. They write a definition in their own words after they have been given enough time and information to formulate meanings. You may also ask students to record an association they have that relates to the word from their own background knowledge or to draw a picture that illustrates the word. Figure 3.4 offers a simple format that students can use to organize their logs. Place students in small groups periodically to share their vocabulary logs with each other.

Graphic Organizers. Most state departments of education offer examples of graphic organizers, including this site from West Virginia: www.wvde.state.wv.us/strategybank/vocabularygraphic organizers.html. Graphic organizers help students deepen their

3.4 Sample Student Vocabulary Log in English or Social Studies

Your association or connection to a vocabulary word may include songs, books, movies, experiences, or symbols.

Vocabulary word	Definition in my own words	Association or connection	Illustration
Example: Idealism	This is when someone sees the best in something; like seeing the ideal, the perfect, the best it can be.	Idealism for me is when I think about a world where there is no violence or war.	

understandings of words in an engaging manner that appeals especially to students who like to use visuals and graphics.

Graphic organizers become a problem when the teacher gives one organizer to the entire class and has everyone fill it out, worksheet style. Instead, use graphic organizers as a personalized learning tool by offering a variety of organizers and asking students to choose the one that best fits the word and their preferences. Students can work in teams and share their organizers with the class.

One of the most effective graphic organizers for all subject areas is the Frayer Model (Frayer, Frederick, Klausmeier, 1969). See Figure 3.5 for an example of a Frayer chart for the term *absolute value* in middle school math.

Variations of the Frayer Model. The possibilities for using this model are nearly endless. Use these questions as examples of ways you can expand this organizer:

- What does it do?
- How, when, why, and where does it happen?
- What does it smell, feel, taste, sound, or look like?
- What are its benefits?
- What are its costs or problems?

3.5 Example of Frayer Model

Define the word/concept: Absolute Value	**Is different from similar words/ concepts**
Absolute value of a number is its distance from 0 on the number line. The absolute value means that the number will have a positive value because it only refers to the distance it is from 0, either left or right.	The absolute value of a number is not necessarily the same as the number itself.
Examples of this word/concept:	**Nonexamples of this word/concept:**
$\lvert 2 \rvert = 2$ $\lvert -2 \rvert = 2$	(−2), −(−2)

- How can the problems be solved?
- What types exist?
- What is its connotation?
- What are its synonyms? Its antonyms?
- What are its stages?
- What are arguments for it? Against it?
- How would it be illustrated? (Lent, 2009, p. 55)

Figure 3.6 shows an adaptation of the Frayer Model using appropriate questions for the science or geography term *drought*. By giving different terms to the groups and tailoring the questions so that students have to dig into the text for information or apply

3.6 Adaptation of Frayer Model

What is it? Drought	**What are the problems?**
Drought is when a region doesn't receive enough rainfall.	Animals may migrate away from the area, famine may occur, and the eco-system may become imbalanced.
How can the problem be solved?	**What is it like?**
By creating dams, using seawater to irrigate, or cloud seeding	Being very thirsty and having no water to drink

what they have learned, meanings are expanded and learning is deepened.

Concept Ladders. Janet Allen (2007, p. 21) uses a similar approach for words that reflect concepts used in English and social studies such as *injustice, recession,* or *freedom* with a graphic organizer called Concept Ladders. Using this strategy, students climb the ladder to understanding by addressing the prompts that may apply to the concept, such as recording the causes and effects, giving historical and contemporary examples, as well as offering reading connections.

- Concept:
- Causes of:
- Effects of:
- Language associated with:
- Words that mean the same as:
- Historical examples of:
- Contemporary examples of:
- Evidence of:
- Literature/reading connections made:

Create Active Vocabulary Instruction

When students are actively involved in learning, their engagement increases and their chances become greater of achieving flow, that satisfying state where time seems to stop. Try to find ways of creating interactive learning of vocabulary whenever possible.

Provide Experiences. Help students uncover the layers of meanings inherent in words by providing experiences with the concepts rather than dry definitions of words. You can help students actively experience words using the following activities.

- Use experts to help students deeply understand concepts. For example, in a high school economics class, if you want students to conceptualize a bull market, bring in a stockbroker to discuss what factors contribute to a bull market and how it differs from a bear market. When discussing the immune system in science, bring in a doctor who can describe various illnesses that result from a compromised immune system. An architect can show math students how the calculation of angles makes his work accurate. Be sure to allow students the opportunity to ask questions and perhaps interview the guest.

- Show photographs or videos that relate to conceptual terms, such as *freedom of speech* in elementary or middle school social studies, or have students bring in pictures that illustrate the words. Students can organize the photographs into categories under associated words to create a visual word wall. They may also create vocabulary PowerPoint slides that illustrate important words or engage in a blog about concept-rich words such as *ethnocentrism* in high school social studies, *ecosystems* in elementary science, or *complementary event* in math.
- Introduce vocabulary by assigning each student a word that she will "own." That means the student will understand the word inside and out and will be prepared to offer examples, analogies, or easy-to-understand definitions to other students who may be having trouble understanding the term. This strategy is helpful in English classes, especially if students may be reading short stories that have specific settings or deal with cultures that are unfamiliar to them.

Focus Discussions. Engage students in a focused discussion, such as with the word *stereotype,* either as a whole class or within small groups after reading a poem or short story in English. Such discussions may begin with a single word but will soon deepen as students address essential questions or big ideas associated with that word. In addition, when students argue a point, such as "Is racism caused by stereotypes?" they are more likely to understand the layered meanings of the word. Focused discussions work well for concepts such as climate change or nuclear power plants in science or for exploring how to use ratios, intersecting lines, or a Monte Carlo simulation in math. Instead of the typical discussion that revolves around text, focus the discussions around a vocabulary word, term, or concept.

As an example, a high school history teacher collaborated with an English teacher to have students explore the term *puritan ethic* by offering these questions as discussion prompts, one question per small group, and then having students share the gist of their conversations with the entire class.

- Some would argue that today's teens have adopted a philosophy of hedonism in contrast to a *puritan work ethic.* Reply to those who would make this point.
- Which groups of Americans still demonstrate a *puritan ethic*? How does this increase or decrease their chances of achieving the American Dream?
- You have just developed a new company and you want *puritan ethic* in your mission statement. Some on the new board of directors are arguing that this term will not play well with future consumers. Make your point for or against including the term in the company's mission statement.

Use Online Tools. Students can actively pursue the meanings of words by typing the word into an Internet search engine. Divide the list of vocabulary words among teams and, with minimal instructions, let them have at it online. If I conduct a search on *abiotic,* for example, I come up with pages and pages of sites, some reputable, some not. I even found several sites that explain a controversial idea, that the BP oil spill off the coast of Louisiana could be related to an abiotic gusher. Give science students 10 minutes to read about the word *abiotic* online and share their findings with the class. You can use this opportunity to show students how to be skeptical readers of websites and discuss the meaning of words at the same time. See Figure 3.7 for examples of websites where students can engage in active vocabulary study.

3.7 Websites for Vocabulary Study	
Wordle www.wordle.net	Students use this website to create word clouds from the information they provide.
Visuwords www.visuwords.com	Students can use this online graphic dictionary and thesaurus that connects associated words and concepts.
Jeopardy Labs www.jeopardylabs.com	Teachers and students use this site to create jeopardy-like games with words.
VocabAhead www.vocabahead.com	Students use this website, associated with SAT prep, to watch videos that explain words.
Quizlet http://quizlet.com	Students and teachers access this website to create digital vocabulary flash cards.

Help Students Acquire Vocabulary Independently

Explicit vocabulary instruction is necessary to help students access difficult text and concepts, but we want them to become independent word learners as well. That means students must learn what to do when they come upon a word they don't know. The goal is that they start acting as proficient readers and make decisions about a word instead of waiting to see if the teacher puts the word on a list. Model for students how to approach new words in the textbook and reassure them that they are capable of being in charge of their own reading and learning. It is a step in the right direction for students to simply stop when they come upon a new word and think about it, even if they decide to skip it and go on.

In a 7th grade social studies textbook, for example, *apartheid* appears. Although the teacher will probably teach this word as a part of vocabulary study in the chapter on Africa, you can show students how to determine for themselves whether they should stop and examine the word or keep on reading.

Students probably need to know the word if it is

- Highlighted in the text.
- Listed as an important word at the beginning of the chapter.

- Pointed out by the teacher.
- Linked to other information in online text.
- Used in a heading.
- Used in an illustration, graph, problem, or photograph.
- Repeated several times in the text.
- Used in an analogy.

Students may not need to remember the word if it is

- Used only once in the text.
- Used to identify a specific person or place that is not critical to the text.
- A technical or foreign term that does not seem to be essential to the main ideas in the text.
- Mentioned but not explained.

With the earlier example, *apartheid,* a student may not be able to pronounce the word, but she would read that it is compared with *segregation* in the United States, an important concept that she has studied in previous years. She would also see a picture of Nelson Mandela, and even if she did not know who he is, she would read in the caption that he spent years in prison for opposing apartheid. A thoughtful student would probably figure out that this is an important word, even if her teacher had not previewed it before reading the chapter. The skill of determining what's important in the text, even in vocabulary study, will transfer to all reading, and it is one that should be reinforced in every class.

Expose Students to Words Through Supplemental Reading

Nearly every vocabulary researcher endorses this one easy method for helping students acquire new vocabulary: reading. Perhaps William Nagy said it best: "What is needed to produce vocabulary growth is not more vocabulary instruction, but more reading" (1988, p. 3). The more students read about topics that are important to the content, the better they will understand the content overall. Read to them from articles or books that you read, create a classroom library related to your discipline, and expose them to words that support the content-area learning. Here are other ways to build students' vocabularies in your content area.

Create diverse classroom libraries. Immerse students in words by providing every opportunity for them to read about topics related to your discipline. Require that students read at home or give them opportunities for independent reading during class. As you read books or articles that you intend to place in your classroom library, underline or highlight words that you want students to pay attention to, or ask them to keep a vocabulary log of new words they come upon while reading. As a team-teacher in a U.S. government/English class, we bombarded students with information from all sorts of sources. Soon, they were reading articles on their own and, as a valuable byproduct, increasing their vocabularies.

Engage in read-alouds. Reading aloud to students exposes them to words that they may not be able to read themselves and deepens their content knowledge. Middle school science teachers, for example, have found their students enjoy listening to them read Caroline Cooney's *Code Orange* (2007), a novel about smallpox that also builds background knowledge about cells. *The Curious Incident of the Dog in the Night-Time* (Hadden, 2004) is told from an autistic child's point of view. He happens to be a math genius as well, so students in middle and high school math can hear math vocabulary while listening to a good story. *One Crazy Summer* (Williams-Garcia, 2011) is great for elementary social studies students as they "sit in" on a Black Panther event.

Make students aware of words. Word consciousness, according to Michael Graves, is "a keen awareness of words and a keen interest in them" (2005, p. 32). Help students become aware of words by making vocabulary a living part of your classroom instruction. Create vocabulary walls. Have students look for websites, political cartoons, headlines, song lyrics, or blogs related to the topic of study and post them on a "Read This!" wall. You can also use interactive word walls about specific topics where students add to the word's meanings with pictures, analogies, or unusual definitions.

Vocabulary Study: Time Well Spent

I know that activities presented in this chapter take a lot of time out of a jam-packed curriculum, but remember that research has shown vocabulary to be the single most important factor contributing to reading comprehension. If you want students to comprehend the content in the textbook and other content-rich sources, to truly understand your subject, there is no better way to spend instructional time than by immersing them in rich and extensive vocabulary study.

Community of Practice: Thoughtful Vocabulary Study

This Community of Practice focuses on effective vocabulary practices and how to use them in the classroom. Any group that collaborates on vocabulary instruction has a relatively easy task that will reap great rewards in student comprehension and engagement. Following is a suggested outline for the group's activities.

In the meeting

1. As a group, review the vocabulary lists for the next unit or chapter that you will teach and tier the words into categories.
2. Discuss strategies on how you will teach words that students need to know. Choices include the following:

- Examine the textbook chapter for graphs, charts, illustrations, or other visual clues that will help students understand the words. Write the page and figure numbers beside appropriate words so you can refer to them when presenting the words to the students.
- Look through the chapter for vocabulary activities. Discuss the effectiveness of each activity in light of the research presented in this chapter. Consider how workable each activity will be for your group of students.

In the classroom

3. Give your students the tier one and tier two words and ask them to fill out a word familiarity chart similar to Figure 3.3. A sample of a student's log appears in Figure 3.4.

4. Use the vocabulary activity with your students (before the next group meeting) and collect the information noted in the next step. Discuss the vocabulary lesson and its effectiveness with others in your group.

In the follow-up meeting

5. Share student data, observational notes, or a video that shows how well students learned new vocabulary based on the chosen activity.

6. Discuss next steps that may include:

- Trying a different vocabulary activity,
- Observing a teacher using a vocabulary activity that was deemed effective,
- Co-teaching a vocabulary lesson, or
- Tweaking the initial activity and using it again.

See Appendix B for lesson study essentials to help you engage in this effective form of professional development.

4

Reading To Learn

My father likes to tell a story about a mule he once knew and respected. Every evening at feeding time, the mule would stop working and head back to the barn. "Stubborn is an understatement," he said. "Old Jack knew when it was time to eat and you could yell, bribe, or pull on his bit with all your might. He was going back to that barn, with or without you." At the risk of offending my colleagues, I must say, with the same admiration that my dad had for his friend Jack, that we educators will do many things that we don't necessarily want to do—and I'm sure working the fields wasn't Jack's idea of a good time—but there are times when we simply dig in our heels.

What does this analogy have to do with a chapter about reading?

I became an English teacher because I loved literature and language and I wanted to help students fall in love with books in the same way that I had when I first read *Black Beauty* (Sewell, 2011) and found myself transported to a world that I had not known existed. But even as a teacher who values reading more than any skill I have ever acquired, I was aghast when I was told to go to a conference to become a "teacher of reading." If I was aghast, my colleagues from math, science, and social studies were absolutely apoplectic.

It turns out that this conference was my introduction to generic reading strategies, the same strategies that would soon be rolling into schools across the country like slow-moving thunder. I came to appreciate these strategies once I realized how they helped my students access the literature I loved, but the movement passed over many content-area teachers who, much like my dad's mule, would work hard all day long teaching their subject, but at the end of the day they simply refused to become a teacher of reading.

Every Teacher a Teacher of Content

Now, when I work with teachers on literacy, I never use the term "reading across the curriculum." Instead, I say "reading within the disciplines," and I honor the vast knowledge that content-area teachers bring to their own subjects. What I ask them to do is help students learn to read in those disciplines the way that they learned when they were novices in their field. As Vacca and Mraz explain,

> A historian reads historical text somewhat differently from the way scientists or mathematicians read text in their respective disciplines. Even though the historian, scientist, and mathematician have developed general reading ability, how they adapt that ability to think with texts in their fields of study is essential to learning content-specific topics. (2011, p. 274)

So, let's make clear that it is the job of the reading specialist or reading teacher to help students with reading skills, and it is another job entirely for the content area teacher to show students how to *use* those skills to access the concepts in each individual discipline.

As you read your textbook, read with the eyes of a student instead of as a teacher or expert. As a teacher, the content is probably so familiar to you that you could have written it. You know what it means to "compare and order rational numbers" in math, to "petition the king" in elementary social studies, or to "classify fungi" in high school biology. But as a student, the terms are probably new. Not only is the vocabulary content-specific and thus more difficult, but the writing is often inconsiderate or rude to the reader. How is it rude? It offers insufficient details, makes no attempt at being interesting, and discusses content in a way that is irrelevant and unconnected to students' experiences.

I read a paragraph in a 6th grade science textbook that would put *anyone* to sleep, much less a multitasking, high-energy, hormone-ridden preteen. It was about the composition of air with one percentage after another written in sentences that all began and ended the same way. Nothing in that paragraph would make students the least bit interested in the very substance that keeps them alive. Be alert for such passages and do whatever it takes to save students from hating your content. Many adults admit that they came to dislike a particular subject in school because of the boring way it was presented in textbooks, only to find out later that they have a passion for the living subject. If you are unfortunate enough to have a set of textbooks written in a droning, authoritative voice, you will need to intercede with lots of reading strategies, lots of supplemental text, and lots of hands-on activities.

One Strategy Does Not Fit All

In most teacher edition textbooks, you will find reading activities specific to your content before, during, and after reading. Textbook companies hire talented and experienced researchers, professors, teachers, and content specialists to develop pedagogically sound strategies and activities to accompany nearly every section of the text. Because reading has become a priority funding item for federal and state budgets in the last few decades, textbook publishers made sure it was their top priority as well.

Unfortunately, the challenge remains. Even if the textbook publishers hired Einstein, he couldn't possibility know the background and abilities of your particular group of students. He couldn't know that your 4th period has 35 kids due to a scheduling problem and that these students come to you before lunch and after P.E., are hungry, tired, and anxious to continue the conversations they began in the hall. Nor could he know that what works with 1st period simply doesn't work with 4th period, and you'd like to see anyone try to engage these students in reading about the magic of mitosis. Teaching a reading strategy just because it is next in the textbook does not take into account the many variables that make one class (to say nothing of the individuals within that class) completely different from another. You have to know what strategy to use with specific students and, more important, teach them how to choose and rely on specific strategies as they move toward becoming independent readers.

What Is a Strategy, Anyway?

Strategies are simply methods for helping us accomplish a task. There are strategies for cooking, for playing sports, for remembering your multiplication tables, for raising children. When applied to reading, they are "intentional plans that readers use to construct independent thought" (Tovani, 2011, p. 180). The beauty of strategies is that when you find the right one, it makes life a lot easier; you just don't have to struggle so hard to succeed. On the other hand, using a strategy whether it works or not, whether it is appropriate to the task or not, is a waste of time and may even take you in a direction you don't want to go. Furthermore, one strategy may work for one person at one time and then may prove utterly useless the next time—depending upon the context and the task. The goal is for students to become *strategic* readers in each discipline.

Students become strategic readers by thinking about their reading, knowing when they aren't comprehending, and figuring out what to do about it. "Strategic learners know what, how, when, and why it is important to monitor what they are reading and to regulate their use of comprehension strategies" (Vacca & Mraz, 2011, p. 275). In the end, teachers cannot make those decisions for students. What they can do is teach them that reading is making sense of the text, not just using the text to answer literal questions or match facts on a test. In short, reading is all about thinking, and strategies are all about internalized scaffolds for helping us with that process.

Harvey and Daniels discuss the advantages of teaching students a "repertoire of strategies they apply flexibly according to the demands of the reading tasks and texts they encounter" and cite research that "students who were taught a group of strategies performed better than those receiving more traditional instruction." They go on to say that multiple strategy instruction not only facilitates comprehension but actually transfers to standardized test performance (2009, p. 26).

Strategies Specific to Disciplines

We know a repertoire of reading strategies benefits our students, so the questions become: Which strategies do you teach students? Which activities out of the hundreds in the teacher editions do you use with students? If you used every reading activity suggested by the editors you would, indeed, become a teacher of reading instead of a teacher of science, social studies, math, or English. It helps to remember that generic reading strategies are not what you are seeking; you want strategies that will help students in *your* content area. The goal is always to help students comprehend text as scientists, historians, writers, poets, or mathematicians so they can better comprehend concepts in each of these areas. Susan Lenski suggests basic differences in how content-area teachers focus on teaching reading:

> The focus of English teachers is on teaching students how to use literary devices to interpret complex fictional texts; mathematics teachers show students how to read texts

> with precision; science teachers demonstrate how to transform information from one form to another; and history teachers should show how to evaluate sources and analyze and evaluate evidence. (2011/2012, p. 279)

I suggest you go further than Lenski by working with others in your discipline, even across grade levels, and have a dialogue about how professionals in your content area read text. Once you're clear about the skills students need to read text in your content area, then you are ready to go through your textbook and highlight strategies that you think will be most useful to students. See the suggested activities for your learning community at the end of this chapter.

How to Choose Effective Reading Strategies and Activities

In considering textbook activities or strategies, give preference to those that reinforce the habits of proficient readers. Harvey and Goudvis (2007) target five strategies that proficient readers use, often subconsciously. Note that these strategies are used both with online and print text. The best reading strategies and activities scaffold and reinforce proficient readers' habits of

1. Making connections. Look for activities that help students make some sort of connection from what they are reading to something with which they are familiar, such as using native plants to make a garden in science or creating a budget in math. Building and activating background knowledge also helps readers make connections.

2. Asking questions. Look for inquiry activities that push students to be curious readers and thinkers rather than passive recipients of information. Many textbooks offer projects including debates, interviews, or web quests. These are all good ways to help students think using questions.

3. Visualizing and making inferences. Look for activities that help students extend their learning beyond the written word by making predictions or imagining possibilities. Seek activities that help them deeply comprehend by reading between the lines and by employing literacies that they use outside of school, especially those that have strong visual components and involve cell phones or the Internet.

4. Determining what is important and separating that from what is less important. Look for activities that help students find and *use* information so they can see why it is important. Discard assignments that have students simply write the main idea of every section. Look for questions that begin with "why" or have them change headings into "why" questions and see if the answer is in the passage.

5. Summarizing and synthesizing. This skill is especially important in using digital textbooks where students must pull together information from a variety of sources and make sense of it. Look for activities that engage students in summarizing content, especially online content, in active ways such as creating a summary with a partner or using a summary to make a point in a presentation. Graphic organizers are good tools for developing these skills as well.

When and How to Teach a Strategy

The best *time* to teach a strategy is when you think students may need to use it. Having every teacher in the school teach a particular strategy on a particular day relegates the strategy to worksheet status and doesn't help students understand the purpose of the strategy. If your students are having difficulty with the concept of seismic waves in middle or high school science, for example, give students graphic organizers and show them where to record the most important ideas about different types of seismic waves, along with illustrations to help them visualize the concept. No doubt the teacher materials from your textbook have appropriate templates of graphic organizers, but if not, go to http://edhelper.com/teachers/graphic_organizers.htm/.

The best *way* to teach a strategy is explicitly, with plenty of modeling. As Judith Langer reminds us:

> Subject-area teachers, who are disciplinary experts, need to guide, model, and provide opportunities for students to try out and step into the ways of thinking that are appropriate to that discipline. They can give students a chance to use disciplinary language and thought in ways that help them refine their understandings and gain knowledge. Teachers can help students become literate thinkers in the various academic disciplines. (2010, p. 14)

The following tips may be useful as you teach reading strategies.

Comprehension strategies. If your students need help with comprehending the text, try to find a strategy that's appropriate in the reading section of your teacher's edition, embedded within the chapter materials for teachers, or in a professional book for teachers. Explain the basic strategy to your students along with how and when a reader might use it *in your discipline*. Reassure students that adult readers also use reading strategies, even if it is a subconscious part of their reading process. Tell students that the more they use the strategy, the more natural it will become. Provide analogies that they can relate to, such as the more you practice your backhand in tennis the better you play and the less you consciously think about the proper way to hold the racket.

Strategy chart. As you introduce new reading strategies, make a strategy chart for students to refer to and have them describe the strategy in their own words in their learning logs.

Demonstrate. Show students how you would use the strategy with a textbook passage. Ask them if they can think of ways to modify the strategy or even rename the strategy to encourage their ownership. For example, they may name a questioning strategy "Stop-Think-Question." Don't fall into the trap of testing students on the specifics of the strategy or making them memorize steps in the strategy. The idea is for students to adapt it to their own needs.

Practice. Have students practice using the strategy with sections from the textbook. Allow them to work with learning partners or in small groups so they can become intrinsically motivated to complete the activity.

Remind. As students read text during the rest of the course, point out when different strategies may be helpful and provide enough time for them to use the strategies.

How to Help Students Read to Learn

"Before, during, and after" is a good mantra for teaching students to read any text in your discipline. When we introduce a new concept, it is important to address each of these areas so students are not only prepared to read but also capable of reading often challenging text.

Before Reading: Invite Students Into the Text

Before reading, students should be invited into the text while teasing their curiosities. Assigning students material without any introduction usually creates a classroom of frustrated, bored readers whose primary goal is living through the class. Take a look at this list and try to do one or more of the following before even thinking about asking students to dive into textbook reading.

- Help students develop curiosity about the topic before reading by doing a chapter walk-through and focusing on visual text features. As you preview the chapter together, encourage students to come up with questions and write them on chart paper (or ask a student to take over this task). As the study progresses, have students check off the questions that have been answered and do research on the ones that weren't addressed in the text.
- Find a young adult novel, picture book, nonfiction article, or surprising facts related to the topic and read parts or the entire text out loud to students to elicit interest.
- Invite a guest speaker to introduce the topic or take students on a virtual field trip to help them gain background knowledge about the subject.

- Introduce key vocabulary in a new way, such as by showing illustrations or photographs related to the words.
- Approach the topic by having students come at it from a problem-solving stance. Tell them they are on a committee that will study the information (in the text) and then make a recommendation to another entity about a hypothetical problem.
- Give students headings or subheadings used in the chapter. Have them write one thing they think they know about the information that will be covered under the heading and one thing they would like to find out. If time permits, divide the headings among small groups of students and have them do research on their heading before they begin reading and share what they discovered with the class.

During Reading: Help Students Become Active Readers

The best thing you can do for students during reading is to help them become active rather than passive readers. Although many of the behaviors in Figure 4.1 may simply look like the difference between a student engaged in school and one who is disengaged, it is important to see these habits through the lens of the reader. Active readers aren't only engaged, they are actually *participating* in the process of reading. Disengaged readers may be able to read well, assuming that they have no underlying problem with reading that should be addressed by a reading specialist, but they haven't developed the habits of proficient readers. Content-area teachers who have not been specifically trained in reading will find Figure 4.1 helpful as they informally assess and analyze students' reading behaviors. Consider giving the chart to students as well so they can engage in a bit of metacognition about their own reading.

Recognize active reading activities in textbooks. As you look for reading activities within the textbook, discard those that *appear* to be active, perhaps with colorful headings, such as

4.1 Characteristics of Active and Passive Readers

Active Readers	Passive Readers
Believe in their own ability to read and understand text.	Doubt their ability to understand text, often even before reading begins.
Know when they aren't comprehending and ask for help or use strategies appropriately.	Don't seem to be aware of when they aren't comprehending and keep on reading without understanding.
Have a pen in hand to make notes (perhaps using sticky notes) or use a highlighter on their own copies.	Don't seem to know what is important to highlight or what notes to make about the text.
Ask questions of the author, themselves, their peers, and their teacher.	Have difficulty formulating questions related to the text and will often say they have no questions when asked.
Can summarize what they have read and have opinions about the content.	Often allow their minds to wander during reading and can't create a logical summary. They offer few opinions about the content.
Make relevant connections to other texts, world events, and personal experiences.	Don't see a connection between one text and another and have difficulty relating the ideas in the text to world events or their own lives.
Think about what's coming next, perhaps making predictions.	Don't predict or anticipate what's coming next.
Set goals that may include using or adapting information in the text for other courses or purposes.	Set a goal of only finishing the reading or completing the assignment.
Make inferences, understand the author's purpose, and "get" other subtleties inherent in the text, such as tone or bias.	Often read word-by-word and look for answers to questions posed by the textbook or teacher rather than internalizing meaning.
Understand that different texts are read in different ways (especially in content areas) and are able to adapt reading skills to the specific text.	Approach all texts the same way.

"Reading with a Purpose," "Dipping into Prior Knowledge," or "Connect!" but are, in fact, low-level questions disguised as innovative reading strategies. In one teacher's edition, for example, I found questions under such headings throughout the chapter that usually began with the words "Ask students." What followed were simply questions designed for the teacher to ask the entire class. As has been standard practice in textbooks for years, "Possible Responses" followed.

Having students stop reading and think about the content is a step in the right direction, but all publishers have done is moved questions from the back of the chapter to a different place in the textbook. The model of teachers asking questions to the whole class should be used infrequently if we are hoping to engage students in active reading and thinking. In contrast, a current algebra textbook has a section titled "Talk Math," and the instructions do, indeed, prompt students to talk to one another about a practice or a skill.

Model how to ask questions. Teach students to read with questions in their heads rather than always seeking answers to scripted questions. A simple activity is to ask them to read a section and, as they read, come up with three questions they would like to ask about anything in the text. Ironically, when you first do this, students may come up with the same type of textbook questions they have been answering. Encourage them to be creative with their questions, focusing on what they really want to know. They may even have questions for which there are no answers. In groups, have them share their questions and come to consensus on one burning question and write it on chart paper. Post the charts on walls and as students read individually and find answers, they may jot the answers on sticky notes to be placed on charts later. If some questions are not answered, it's time for some online research or perhaps time to decide that the question is not pertinent.

Readers who ask questions are showing evidence of comprehension. They are engaging in the process of constructing meaning, finding answers, solving problems, and clarifying their thinking (Harvey & Goodvis, 2007). What's more, David Pearson notes that "The questions a student asks after reading a text are a better assessment than the questions that a student can answer about a text" (2010).

Although children spend most of their young lives asking questions as a strategy for understanding their own environment,

4.2 Using Questions to Deepen Meaning in Content Areas

Here are the types of questions that students can use when they question each other:

- Does this make sense to you?
- How would you figure this out?
- Do you understand this word/concept/problem/map?
- What is the next step/phase/event?
- Do you agree with this?
- Do you remember studying about . . .?
- How does this connect to . . .?

Here are the types of questions that students may use when they question the author:

- What is the author saying here?
- What does the author *mean* by this?
- Why does the author choose to put that piece of information here?
- How does this fit in with what the author has told us before?
- Why does the author choose this particular word, phrase, or concept?

Here are the types of questions students may use to question themselves:

- Why am I confused about this part?
- How can I figure out the meaning of this word?
- Whom can I ask to help me clarify this concept?
- Should I reread this section, problem, or paragraph to help me understand it?
- Do I agree with what I have just read?
- How can I make a connection to help me remember what I've read?
- How important is this idea/concept/word/step?

Here are the types of questions that teachers may use to question themselves:

- How can I elicit longer, more elaborate answers?
- How can I encourage students to engage in a discussion with each other rather than talking only to me?
- How can I keep students engaged with questions that are meaningful and relevant?
- How can I make sure students are not simply parroting back answers from the text without any depth of understanding?
- How can I incorporate student questions into my lesson?

once they get to school they quickly shift to question-answerers. Students have to be retaught how to ask questions, especially in the upper grades. Figure 4.2 contains a chart that may help you and your students begin thinking interrogatively once again.

Allow students to practice asking questions by providing provocative articles that interest them and are related to the topic. Since middle school teachers are used to being grossed out by their students, I often give them an article about the proliferation of bed bugs and ask them to talk with their group members and come up with questions about these facts:

- Bedbugs can survive without food 550 days.
- There were 4,088 bedbug infestations in New York City in 2009, but only 82 in 2004.
- One in 5 Cincinnati residents experienced bed bugs this year (Von Drehle, 2010).

Textbooks also offer sidebars of interesting information that can be used to help students develop questioning skills. Here are some great books with short pieces of interesting text that you can use to help students with questioning skills.

- *Freakonomics: A Rogue Economist Explores the Hidden Side of Everything* (Levitt and Dubner, 2009, 315 pages) for middle and high; all subjects
- *Oh, Yuck! The Encyclopedia of Everything Nasty* (Masoff, 2000, 224 pages) for science; elementary and middle
- *Oh, Yikes! History's Grossest, Wackiest Moments* (Masoff, 2006, 308 pages) for social studies; elementary and middle
- *When Do Fish Sleep and Other Imponderables of Everyday Life* (Feldman, 2005, 320 pages). Feldman has written a series of similar books for all ages.

Teach notetaking. Help students become active readers by using a two-column note-taking system. Pick and choose among prompts shown in Figure 4.3 and make up your own to keep students interested and actively engaged with the reading.

Demonstrate talking back to the text. Cris Tovani tells her students that the best strategies "are the ones that help readers 'talk back to the text' " (2011, p. 180). When students talk back to text they are actively reading, so we need to give them plenty of opportunities to talk to the text and to others about the text. See Chapter 5 for ideas about how to get students "talking" to text in

4.3 Examples of Two-Column Notes

Use the following prompts to help students learn to think about what they are reading. Have students divide their papers in half by drawing a vertical line down the middle of the page. In the first column, ask students to respond to one or more prompts appropriate to the reading selection. Especially at first, you may need to assign the prompts. In the second column, ask students to elaborate on their response or answer the question provided. Allow students to share their responses in small groups after completing their charts.

What is important?	What is trivial?
What does the author say?	What does the author mean?
The heading for this section is	A better heading would be
This quote:	Makes me think:
The most important sentence in this section is:	Because
This paragraph	Could be summarized as
The big idea is	The details are
The problem is asking me to	The most important words in this problem are
This concept	Looks like this (illustrate):
What the character did (summarized below)	Is/is not what I would have done because
This event	Is more significant than others because
This happened	because
I think the author has a bias	because

writing. Responding to text may be as simple as asking a student to turn to her learning partner and tell him what she thinks about the text in a specific way, such as "When did you feel that a friend had your back the way the character did in the story?" or "Tell your partner why you think there's a photograph of the particle accelerator in the book? How does it help you understand the text?" Their discussions can be very brief, often only a minute or so, but such a practice gives the kids a break from reading and helps them to hone their understanding. It also teaches them that reading is an active, not a passive activity.

Allow opportunities for discussions. We know that when students discuss information, it helps them construct and clarify meaning, just as it does for adults. So students who are studying the Industrial Revolution need to talk about how the advantages and disadvantages of industrialization shaped the United States and share their thoughts with others in the class.

Many schools are taking advantage of videoconferencing to allow their students to engage in discussions with students from classrooms around the world. High school students at South Plantation High School in Florida were in a videoconference with peers in Egypt when President Mubarak stepped down. Students were able to talk with each other about this historic event. "Educators say the collaborations, which lend themselves to co-curricular projects, foster deep and meaningful conversations, whet a thirst for knowledge that textbooks cannot offer, and show that people in different countries have a lot more in common than many assume" (Flanigan, 2012, p. 1).

Unfortunately, too many classrooms are places where teachers do most of the talking and students do most of the listening. It should be the other way around. This problem is exacerbated because many textbooks offer written assignments but few choices for intermittent or deep discussion—much less suggestions for videoconferencing. In one 3rd grade social studies textbook I did find a great feature titled Talk About It. Some of the prompts were less than engaging, but others were good discussion starters, such as the one that asked students to discuss what they thought about the Cherokees uniting as a tribe in 2009 after 25 years. Imagine how much more engaging this topic could have been if students had videoconferenced with Native American students in North Carolina, for example, especially if their teacher provided a current events article such as "Cherokee Reunion Celebrates Heritage" (Copeland, 2009). Similarly, English textbooks often have sections that give suggestions on how to engage students in literature circles or inquiry groups. These activities are often good, as long as you've taken the time to model what the activity looks like before sending students off to work together.

Benefits of Discussions. Hammond and Nessel (2011) provide benefits from peer interaction directly related to comprehension, including

- Discussion improves retention: "When students discuss . . . they are more likely to retain the information and be able to retrieve it later" (p. 87).
    - Have students talk about challenging word problems with their learning partners before solving a word problem and then again after they think they have solved it.
- "Discussion shapes cognition. . . . Even a typical discussion of a reading selection has a significant impact on participants' cognition" (p. 87).
    - In 7th grade science, have students discuss why a low caloric diet is considered healthy and what one would look like.
- "Collaborative efforts enhance the breadth and depth of comprehension. . . . Conversation yields more robust understanding for all" (p. 88).
    - Have students in an elementary social studies class discuss what it would have been like to have been a Pony Express rider after reading about that time period in history.
- Interaction improves students' capacities for thinking: "As students learn to weigh each other's contributions, they become more discerning and more adept at thinking" (p. 88).
    - After students read about the life of Muhammad Ali in a high school English textbook, have them discuss the validity of boxing critics' points that such a sport encourages violence in our society.

Look for textbook activities that give students an opportunity for discussion, either in small groups or with a partner, but make sure that the directions aim their discussions at furthering their understanding of the text. If you don't see any such activities, create them, especially with the help of your learning community, and incorporate them into your lessons.

After Reading: Help Students by Choosing the Best Activities

One of the hardest parts of using textbooks is deciding which of the many activities provided at the end of the chapter you should use. It is admittedly much faster and less messy to have students only answer textbook questions, but we know they will understand and retain information better if they are actively involved in learning. As you will read in the chapter on assessment (Chapter 6), I argue that putting students through the typical textbook standardized test practice is cruel and unusual punishment—as well as counterproductive to long-term understanding and engagement.

Let's take a look at a typical chapter in a 5th grade science textbook on using natural resources. There are seven activities offered after students have read only four pages of text. One is a low-level comprehension question (which could be used by partners for a quick "Turn to your partner and respond to this question" activity), two are writing prompts, three are research activities, and one is a creative project related to the topic. Clearly, students can't do all the activities, but the textbook has done the heavy lifting by providing differentiated assignments that can be divided among students and shared with the entire class. You could allow students to choose the task that will best demonstrate their understanding of the content, or you could place students in groups based on their needs. In any event, imagine how much students would learn about their topic (and how many standards you would cover) if they engaged in just one of these activities and shared their work with the rest of the class. With a little adaptation, you can make some of the activities provided in a 5th grade textbook on using natural resources more interesting for the students and better fit your teaching goals. Adaptation is a practice I strongly recommend to all content area teachers when using textbook assignments.

- Write an article for a newspaper, blog, or website about how governments in some countries are trying to preserve their natural environments.

- Write a letter to a conservation group or oil company about why you will or will not one day invest in a car that uses alternative fuels.
- Research some of the organizations that work to protect marine ecosystems. Give a multimedia presentation to the class about the work of a specific organization.
- Search alternative fuel sources online, such as ethanol, wind power, or solar power. Explain to the class how the United States and other nations are developing such energy sources.
- Create a poster or brochure that shows how people can protect natural environments in their community.
- Research what other countries are doing to decrease their dependency on foreign oil imports. Present a debate to the class about whether these strategies will succeed.

And What if They Can't Read?

All these activities and strategies have avoided one important question. What do we do when students simply can't read the text? We can help students comprehend by showing them how to become aware of when they are not getting it and then teaching them strategies to monitor their comprehension and do something to repair meaning. They may reread, ask someone to read with them, slow down (or stop) their reading, skip parts and continue reading to see if meaning becomes clear, or look at text features such as illustrations or graphs to help with clarification. You can model all of these strategies while teaching your content the first few weeks of school.

You can also help students increase their self-efficacy in reading by assuring them we all could eventually find a text that would prove too difficult for us to easily comprehend. Tell them about reading income tax forms, insurance policies, or, for me, a book by Stephen Hawking. I might be able to pronounce all the words, but it would take me a while to deeply comprehend what I am reading. I tell students honestly that the anxiety of thinking I might have to take a test after reading a chapter in Hawking's book would completely obliterate my self-efficacy before I even began. Self-efficacy, as I discussed in Chapter 1, is essential for helping students achieve. Unfortunately, many students will relate to a cycle similar to the one in Figure 4.4.

Guthrie argues that providing struggling readers with texts that are near their "already deficient reading levels" will not improve their skills. In fact, he says, "it will only sustain the achievement gap" (2008, p. 71). Richard Allington's article "You Can't Learn Much From Books You Can't Read" nails the issue. "It seems so obvious—students need textbooks that they can actually read" (2002, p. 16). Believing that students *should* be able to read grade-level texts sounds right in theory, but we have to deal with what *is,* as we learned the first day we walked into a classroom. Remember, too, that just because kids can't read doesn't

4.4 Cycle of Failure for Students Who Struggle with Reading

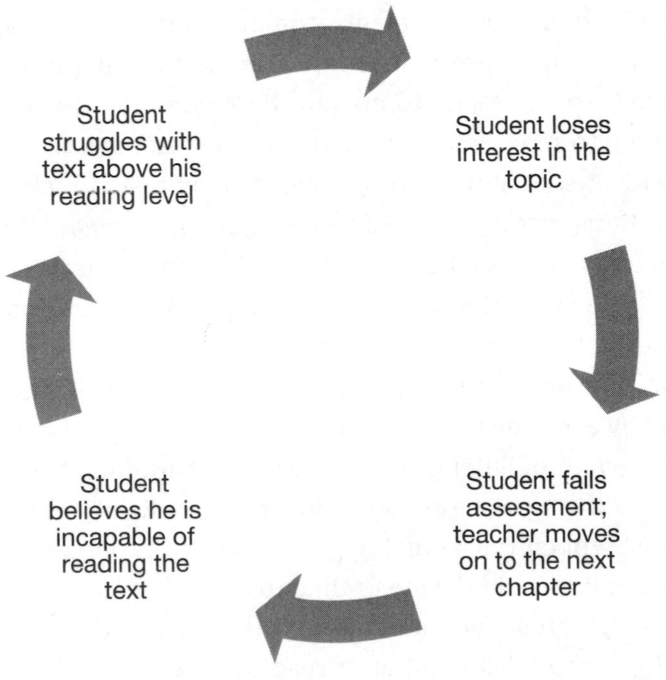
Student struggles with text above his reading level
Student loses interest in the topic
Student fails assessment; teacher moves on to the next chapter
Student believes he is incapable of reading the text

mean they can't think. They may not be able to read fluently, at least in your content area, but they may be more than capable of thinking through complex ideas. You can support these students' understandings in your discipline simply by providing texts they *can* read while scaffolding understanding and valuing their contributions in discussions and projects.

Differentiated Texts

For many content-area teachers, the idea of having students read different texts may be a scary one. Once you get the hang of it, you'll find increased interest and motivation in students who struggle with reading. In fact, teachers report that students who have discipline problems often become engaged, even enthusiastic, about a topic—and they become better readers—simply by *reading* rather than pretending to read a text they can't access. Chapter 7 goes into more depth about how to find supplemental texts for students on all levels, but following are ideas for turning your classroom into one where all students are reading, whether it is a word problem, a historical document, or a poem.

- Informally assess students' reading abilities by having them read aloud individually to you, take a basic comprehension test (teacher or textbook created) after reading a piece of text, or provide a summary of a section of text. You will gain valuable information about which students struggle with the text, which ones can comprehend but need more time, and which ones are proficient readers.
- Look for old textbooks in your discipline on various grade levels in your district's book depository. You can provide different books with similar content to different groups in your class. Facilitating discussions (or having students discuss text in small groups) will fill in gaps for those who are reading easier texts.
- Go online and find articles on topics you teach that kids may find easier to read. The first year you collect such articles is the hardest, but soon you and your learning community will amass a bank of articles at various grade levels on every topic.

The students' resultant learning will make it worth the effort. This works especially well in science and history, where current articles are written on a variety of reading levels.

- Ask your media specialist to provide a text set of books and materials on the same topic at various reading levels (see Chapter 7).
- Allow students to read to a partner or read in small groups to aid their comprehension and increase their self-efficacy. This works well when students are reading a difficult short story, say by an author from an earlier time period such as O. Henry; trying to understand a complex concept such as gene encoding in science; or working through a math problem that is especially challenging.

Teaching to Learn

Thankfully, we can rely on reading teachers and coaches to help students who have problems learning to read. We can enhance their efforts by giving students positive experiences with texts they *can* read, showing them how to approach challenging texts in our disciplines, and working with each other to find ways of using the textbook to support learning rather than inhibit it.

Community of Practice: Reading to Learn

This Community of Practice will focus on content-area reading. Teachers can work in content-area groups, even across grade levels, as they engage in study and classroom practice. Following is a suggested outline for the group's activities.

In the meeting

1. Spend time discussing specific reading skills needed to comprehend text in your discipline and how those differ from skills needed in other disciplines. List these skills on chart paper and add to them as your study continues.
2. Choose a literacy book in your content area, perhaps from the list at the end of the chapter, and engage in a book study. See Appendix A for book study tips.

Before the next meeting

3. Read agreed-upon assignments.

In the follow-up meeting

4. At the meeting, discuss the concepts presented in your reading and look critically at the next chapter of the textbook that you are teaching. Following are sample discussion questions.

- What do you see as the most significant challenges your students have with textbook reading?
- Which strategies, activities, or new understandings have you gained from your reading?
- In what ways does the textbook address your new learning about content-area literacy? In what ways does it not?
- Which textbook activities or strategies are most effective based on what you have learned from your book study?
- Which activities are feasible considering the time and resources you have available?
- Which parts of the textbook should be skimmed or skipped based on what you know of your students' abilities, background knowledge, the curriculum, and the textbook's approach to the topic?
- Which supplemental materials can you provide to meet the reading levels of all students?

5. Choose a strategy or activity either from the textbook or from the book you are reading and talk through how you will use it or adapt it for use in your classrooms. Participants may choose the same activity or choose different activities and compare their effectiveness.

In the classroom

6. As students engage in the activity, keep observational notes about changes in their reading habits and skills.

7. At the end of specific units, evaluate how the reading strategies or activities improved student learning. Write notes for group discussion.

In the follow-up meetings

8. Discuss your notes and experiences with other participants. Revise your practice based on findings and continue this process for the duration of the book study.

Book Study Resources for Reading to Learn in the Content Areas

Building Literacy in Social Studies: Strategies for Improving Comprehension and Critical Thinking by D. Ogle, R. Klemp, and B. McBride (2007)

Literacy for Real: Reading, Thinking, and Learning in the Content Areas by R. Lent (2009)

Literacy Learning in the Content Areas by S. Kane (2003)

Literacy Strategies for Improving Mathematics Instruction by J. D. Kenney, E. Hancewicz, L. Heuer, D. Metsisto, and C. L. Tuttle (2005)

Reading and Writing in Science: Tools to Develop Disciplinary Literacy by D. Fisher and M. C. Grant (2010)

Reading Better, Reading Smarter: Designing Literature Lessons for Adolescents by D. Appleman and M. Graves (2012)

Teaching Reading in Social Studies, Science and Math by L. Robb (2003)

5

Writing to Learn

During the No Child Left Behind years, content-area teachers didn't worry too much about incorporating writing into their instruction. The focus was almost entirely on reading. I remember arguing passionately to staff at Florida's Department of Education that writing and reading were reciprocal processes and one couldn't be taught to the exclusion of the other. They were all about following the NCLB law, however, so writing was sent packing. And, as I noted earlier, textbook publishers were in the business of making sure states had what they wanted, so that included lots of reading strategies in content-area textbooks and few writing assignments.

That was then. Now, the Common Core State Standards have sent publishers back to the drawing board as they try to find ways to "return writing to its place as one of the basics of education" (Calkins, Ehrenworth, & Lehman, 2012, p. 102). The standards emphasize writing in all disciplines, with a focus on narrative, persuasive, and informational writing. In addition, they are insisting on routine writing in every class and they underscore quality, not just quantity. Teachers have a lot of ground to cover if they hope to meet standards that have elevated writing from an overlooked stepchild to the belle of the ball.

The best place to begin the transformation is through writing to learn because it is such a natural fit in all subject areas. In fact, writing is a vehicle for assimilating information and reinforcing reading skills as well as a perfect mechanism for storytelling, reflection, and argument. The National Writing Project (NWP), an organization that has been studying the effects of writing for the last three decades, concluded definitively that writing develops higher-order thinking skills such as analyzing, synthesizing, evaluating, and interpreting—and that writing also affects comprehension (2006). The *Writing Next* report affirmed their findings by stating, "Writing is a means of extending and deepening students' knowledge; it acts as a tool for learning subject matter" (Graham & Perin 2007, p. 9).

Why does writing increase skills and improve comprehension? Perhaps it is the struggle with getting ideas on paper that helps learners make sense of concepts. As the NWP notes, "The very difficulty of writing is its virtue; it requires that students move beyond rote learning and simply reproducing information, facts, dates and formulae. Students must also learn how to question their own assumptions and reflect critically on an alternative or opposing viewpoint" (2006, pp. 22–23). The National Commission on Writing reinforces this point: "If students are to make knowledge their own, they must struggle with the details, wrestle with the facts, and rework raw information and dimly understood concepts into language they can communicate to someone else. In short, if students are to learn, they must write" (2006, p. 47).

Unfortunately, not all writing accrues the same benefits as writing to learn. Langer and Applebee in their study of how writing shapes thinking explain why this is so.

> Short-answer study questions . . . lead students to focus on particular items of information either located in the

text or implied by it. When completing writing tasks of this sort, students often look for the information in the textbook or in class notes and "transcribe" it directly onto the paper—from text to paper, with the student writer as conduit. Little rethinking of the material usually takes place. (2007, p. 135)

Textbook Writing vs. Writing to Learn

Many textbook writing prompts do not advance the cause of writing to learn. Very few, except perhaps some in English textbooks, even address writing to learn. In a review of textbook writing assignments, I found that most provide three types of writing prompts and that these did not occur within the chapters but as one of many assignments at the unit's end. Textbook assignments generally focus on

- Writing in a creative way to a specific prompt such as creating a brochure, a poster, an advertisement, a timeline, or a speech with the topic clearly defined for students.
- Writing as a way of review, such as summarizing, outlining, or repeating facts or narratives.
- Writing as a straightforward evaluation, which may involve answering factual comprehension questions or writing a brief description, explanation, or summary—the length often designated as one paragraph or from 100 to 300 words.

Examples of typical textbook writing assignments include "Write a paragraph about how global positioning systems improve life for people," "Copy and fill in the graphic organizer to compare and contrast planets," "Write a report on the results of your experiment," or "Tell how one of these books might influence your life." Instead of using writing as a means to help students comprehend, analyze, and internalize information, textbook prompts merely direct students to complete a task, usually with no instruction on *how* to write. What's more, these prompts are almost always task oriented instead of process oriented, an important distinction.

At the end of each chapter in a 7th grade social studies textbook, students are instructed to complete a journal activity, which implies some sort of expressive writing. Instead, each prompt is exactly the same and directs students to demonstrate comprehension by summarizing what was learned. It seems that textbook publishers don't understand that it is through the *process* of writing that deep understanding most often occurs, not through summarizing. To capitalize on the many advantages of writing, students need time to think about content, grapple with its implications, question its validity, formulate responses, collaborate with others, and, perhaps, save the writing in a portfolio to return to later.

When I was working with a 5th grade math teacher, we decided that we wanted to find ways to incorporate *writing to learn* into a lesson with word problems. First, we put students in groups of four and arranged them in a circle around a table. We then gave each group a different, challenging word problem and instructed them to engage in a paper version of what we called a blog-around. The room was totally silent as students read the problem and began freewriting about how they might find a solution. Students wrote on their own papers for four to five minutes until the teacher said, "pass." Each student then passed her paper to the student on her right. With each new piece of paper, the students read what was previously written and then responded in writing for another several minutes before we instructed them to "pass" again. The process continued until, finally, the papers returned to the original writers. Then, in their groups, students discussed how they would present their solution to the class. Not every group solved the problem, but all groups made significant gains in understanding it.

Interestingly, when we read the students' papers, we found that in the first round of writing most students simply summarized the word problem. Many wrote that they didn't know where to begin. By the time they were writing as the fourth responder, a majority of students had figured out the problem—or were well on their way—and they were also able to express in writing how they would attempt to solve it.

Adapt this activity to various content areas by giving students a piece of challenging text and having them blog about it instead of struggling with it as a solitary, silent reading task. Or, you might offer other discipline-specific materials for them to use as resources in understanding the content. In science, for instance, provide a photograph or lab drawing to each group and ask students to write about what they see. You may also give lab notes, a nonfiction article about a new finding, or a hypothesis for students to ponder. Social studies students can write about a primary document, photograph, historical event, or current news piece. In English classes, where students are used to writing extensively, this practice provides a means for collaborative writing, one of the 11 key elements of adolescent writing instruction recommended by Graham and Perin (2007) in their report *Writing Next*.

Reflective Writing-to-Learn Assignments

Writing to learn often takes place when students write reflective pieces about what they are learning and how they are learning, perhaps in a learning log or interactive notebook. Such metacognitive activities help students reflect on how they come to understand challenging texts and allow them the freedom to inquire and discover without fear of a bad grade. Langer and Applebee call such writing "think papers" where there are no right or wrong answers; students simply "progress toward a deeper understanding of the material" (2007, p. 137).

A 6th grade science teacher was amazed at what her students had *not* learned when she asked them to write a reflection piece instead of traditional lab notes. She found that her students could accurately describe what had happened in the lab and that they could measure and record the mass of a bottle of water before and after an effervescent tablet had been dropped into it, but they did not understand that the goal of the lab was conservation of mass. Many students were good at recording data in a table provided in the text, but when asked to write the point of the experiment, they said they didn't know. See Figure 5.1 for

5.1 Self-Reflection Sheet

Student: ______________________

Answer each question as honestly and completely as you can, especially since your answers will not be graded. Remember that learning is an ongoing process and this is another step in understanding yourself as well as continuing to learn about the subject we've been studying.

1. What did you learn from this activity, text, experiment, or unit?
2. What questions do you still have?
3. What was most difficult for you in this assignment? Why?
4. What did you find easiest? Why?
5. If you did the assignment over again, how would you change your work?
6. What new ideas do you have now that you have completed the assignment?
7. How will learning this information help you in your future (as a student or in your career)?
8. What suggestions do you have for your teacher when doing this activity with other students in the future?
9. What learning would you like to someday pursue on your own related to this topic?
10. Any other comments?

an example of a self-reflection sheet that can be used for nearly any unit or lesson in any subject matter.

Remember that assignments asking for whole chapter summaries or directing students to take notes as they read can lead to superficial understandings (Langer & Applebee, 2007). The National Commission on Writing reminds us that "Facility with writing opens students up to the pleasure of exercising their minds in ways that drilling on facts, details, and information never will. More than a way of knowing, writing is an act of discovery" (2006, p. 52). Once again we see the importance of teachers, not textbooks, because teachers can manipulate students' understanding, either superficially or deeply, through the type of writing assignments and support they provide.

Going Beyond the Writing Process

The writing process has been a staple in most English textbooks for years: prewrite, draft, revise, and edit. Content-area teachers are often encouraged to have their students engage in the same process. In fact, the writing process approach is one of the elements recommended in the *Writing Next* report, the National Commission on Writing advocates its use, and it is prominently featured in the Common Core State Standards. The teaching of writing, however, does not rely on one method or one approach, which may be the reason it is so difficult for textbooks to provide satisfactory writing assignments. A research brief from the National Council of Teachers of English affirms that "Writing, especially at the present moment, is complex and difficult to define." The research brief continues by stating that we do know some important things about writing: "It is not created by a singular, linear process; it cannot be taught, like bike riding, as a single skill; it changes with shifting technologies—like today's new media; it can enable and enhance learning; it takes many forms" (2008, p. 3). And those forms look different in various content areas, which is why we must give students many opportunities to write in every class in a variety of ways.

Just as there is no one way to teach writing, there are multiple ways that students can engage in the process. In a National Assessment of Educational Progress and Educational Testing Service study of effective assignments, the reviewers found that "Effective writing assignments encourage student engagement with writing processes in ways that go beyond the formulaic use of prewriting, drafting, and revision" (National Writing Project & Nagin, 2006, p. 47). One high school English textbook, for example, directs students to write a short summary of a nonfiction piece about Oprah Winfrey. Although the assignment includes steps to help students in their writing, the instructions are so prescriptive that students end up merely retelling the article. If teachers had students engage in prewriting, drafting, revising, and editing such a piece, they would moan in boredom—and the result would probably not be much better than their first rough draft. A more effective writing prompt might be to have students choose one of the events that happened in Winfrey's life and write how they would have handled that challenge or why they think Winfrey rose to stardom in spite of such a difficult childhood. Engaging students in content through writing has little to do with a formula; it has everything to do with thinking and communicating through the written word.

Components of Effective Writing Assignments

Although there are many components to effective writing assignments and each assignment differs based on the discipline and topic of study, the National Writing Project recommends four components as a good place to start when evaluating textbook writing assignments or creating new ones: 1) content and scope, 2) organization and development, 3) audience and communication, and 4) engagement and choice (2006, pp. 47–48). Following are explanations of these components as they relate to textbook writing assignments.

Go Beyond Restating the Text

It is worth repeating that an effective assignment goes beyond asking students what they have read or restating the text in their own words. Instead, ask students to take what they have read and apply or transform this information in their writing. Examples include the following:

- Compare characters in one short story to characters in another story based on how they respond to a problem.
- Use climate data for a specific area in the country being studied to determine what crops would grow best there.
- Explain how a formula learned in math could be used in real-world settings.

Effective writing assignments encourage students to use their reasoning abilities, analytical skills, and personal connections to make sense of the content. Students who write to learn can be much more flexible and independent in the way they use writing to transform information into knowledge.

Model How to Organize and Develop Ideas

Strengthen textbook assignments by giving students information about how they can organize and develop their ideas. When you ask students to describe, explain, persuade, or tell about something, make sure you provide enough information in the assignment to guide them in their writing.

Often, writing prompts assume students know how to write about a topic without their ever having being taught how to do it. For example, instead of asking students in a science class to "Write a report to share the results of an experiment with the class" as one textbook directs, ask them to do the following:

> Write a report about your experiment. Include the problem at the beginning of your paper and explain how you arrived at your hypothesis and state it. Describe how you collected data and what observations you made. Then, explain how you arrived at your conclusions.

Giving such an assignment scaffolds the process for students by showing them *how* to write to learn. As always, teachers will need to model first, perhaps writing their own paper about a different experiment in front of students so they understand what is expected.

Provide an Authentic Audience

A writing assignment with a real, not a pretend, audience will engage students in the writing and may inspire them to produce a better piece. A writing assignment with an authentic audience is often the culmination of a learning experience. A 4th grade science text instructs students to write about how they experience motion. In the same text box, an engaging picture of a fair ride swinging kids into the air adds interest and motivation (Harcourt School Publishers, 2009). The writing assignment would be more effective if students were asked to write the account on Facebook or send an e-mail message to a friend or relative in another city describing a ride they enjoyed at the fair. Students could also write about the ride and give the account to a younger student who might not be old enough to get on the ride. Similarly, if students in an English class are studying and analyzing the characteristics of effective speeches, ask them to write a speech and present it to the class. Turning in a written speech for a grade or an analysis of a speech with only the teacher as an audience leads to the "Is this for a grade?" syndrome instead of students taking intrinsic pride in the task.

Authentic audiences for writing assignments include classmates, students in another class or school, or community members who may have an interest in the topic. Social networking sites are also perfect for sharing writing with audiences other than the teacher; students love to create websites, podcasts, or multimedia presentations for their peers. You can take advantage of their inclination to contribute to blogs, wikis, Twitter, or their own Facebook pages as ways of having them write "for real." The website at www.figment.com, similar to Facebook, is an engaging way for writers in middle and high school to publish work. A teacher in Philadelphia said that the website is perfect for her students, noting that "It's important for students to know that their work is viewed by more than just their teacher. This gives them an authentic reason to write" (Palmer, 2012, p. 2). Go to www.zinepal.com and allow students to create printable PDFs or ebooks. An online tool, www.storybird.com, is especially useful for elementary grades, where students can write their own books. They could also turn their writing into a letter to the editor or to a favorite author. Simply posting student writing on a bulletin board or publishing it in a three-ring binder or booklet for others to read increases motivation for writing.

Offer Students Choices

As noted in Chapter 1, choice is an important component of engagement in any task, but, unfortunately, textbooks rarely give choice. Except in English texts, there is generally a short assignment directing the students to write in a prescribed manner. In a current 4th grade social studies text, I did find a section that gave students a choice of writing a poem, a conversation, or a newspaper article. It is too bad that such choices are only given at the end of each unit, however, instead of at the end of each chapter.

If you decide to add choices to those provided in the textbook, there is one caveat. Give students a reasonable number of choices for their writing—not too many to overwhelm them and not too few to restrict the flow of their thinking and writing. A middle school English teacher was excited about allowing her students complete freedom in choosing a topic to research and write about. After the project's completion, students reflected on the process. The teacher was surprised to find that students felt frustrated by what they perceived as a lack of direction and suggested that she provide a more narrow range of choices for the next group of students. One way to give students choice and address their interests is to have students keep a page in their learning logs for writing ideas. As they read about a topic or engage in discussions, they can jot down thoughts they would like to explore, investigate, or think about. Then, when it's time to write, they will have a tailored list of topics from which to choose.

An important part of writing is discovering what you want to say—and how to say it. In looking for good writing assignments in textbooks or creating your own, try to give students as many opportunities as possible to formulate their own thoughts as they become proficient and comfortable with the process of writing in your discipline.

Tools for Content-Area Writing

Tools used for writing transcend disciplines and media. Just as Facebook and blogs have transformed "out of school" literacies, writing tools can change students' perceptions of "in school" writing and, at the same time, help them become better (and more fluent) writers. Students can create and store writing on their own computers, in the cloud, or in physical notebooks, but it is the act of writing that reinforces learning in all subject areas.

Interactive Notebooks or Learning Logs

Teachers have had students keep notebooks for years, but the concept of an interactive notebook is a bit different. An interactive notebook is one that students have access to every day, a place where they not only store their work but actually *do* their work. It is a place of reflection, a place to experiment, a place to share ideas with learning partners. It contains tangible proof of learning and all the starts, stops, and reversals that make up that mysterious process.

A friend once told me that her son had an interest in trains, even as an adolescent. She marveled at the way he kept a notebook in which he placed articles about trains and their histories, wrote about trains, created timelines of related information, and illustrated the pages with trains and things related to trains. Some little girls do the same thing with horse notebooks and many adults keep scrapbooks on a variety of topics. Interactive notebooks can be used in a similar way, and if students take ownership of their notebooks, they are much more likely to use them while learning. The knowledge they incorporate into their notebooks becomes theirs rather than something imposed on them. Kellie Marcarelli describes how such a tool works for her students:

> An interactive notebook is a tool students use to make connections prior to new learning to revise their thinking, and to deepen understandings of the world around them. It is the culmination of a student's work throughout the year that shows both the content learned (input) and the reflective knowledge (output) gained. Put another way, an interactive notebook provides a space where students may take what is inside their brains, lay it out, make meaning, apply it and share it. (2010, p. 2)

Stephanie Anderson, a middle school science teacher in Michigan, told me that her students have been using interactive notebooks for years. She finds new ways to make them interactive with each group of students. In a recent unit on the effects of fracking, she gave students a choice in how they demonstrated those effects in their notebooks. Her students had learned to use notebooks for active learning, so they quickly created raps, illustrations, comic strips, and poems in their notebooks. For everyday lessons, they draw a vertical line down the notebook page. One side is for input from the teacher or text and the other side—directly across from that input—is for output or where students record what they understand about the content in ways that makes sense to them. Ms. Anderson said the notebook is one of the most valuable learning tools her students use.

The interactive notebook or learning log can be used in any content-area class each day and integrates writing as a fundamental part of learning. Students would have a different notebook for each subject, which would include content-specific items such as the following.

- Graphic organizers
- Writing assignments
- Lab notes
- Questions about their reading and learning—*not* short answers to comprehension questions
- Opinions, arguments, responses, or other expressive writing
- Group writing projects, including "blog-around" papers
- Analysis of primary documents
- Lists of vocabulary (found on their own)
- Grammar rules
- Summaries of articles, blogs, or tweets related to a topic
- Illustrations, poems, cartoons, storyboards, photographs
- Foldables
- Lists of books they have read or want to read and reading logs
- Notes from small group discussions
- Analysis of word problems
- Exit slips, entrance slips, quick writes
- Self-reflection pieces

For a list of questions that can be used to help spur students' self-reflection, refer once again to Figure 5.1. Ask students to write self-reflection pieces either daily or weekly, as it fits into the flow of your classroom.

Journals

Journals differ from learning logs and notebooks in that they encourage expressive rather than analytical writing. In a hands-on study conducted by two biology teachers, they found that such writing helps improve retention of information. An experimental group of students used expressive writing as a way to think through problems by keeping reading and writing logs, writing to an audience other than the teacher, and participating in group writing. The teachers concluded that students who had the opportunity to use expressive writing understood the material better than the control group (National Writing Project & Nagin, 2006, pp. 52–53).

Make sure each student has a personal journal, either a paper notebook or an electronic version, such as a blog. If students have Internet access, you can try http://penzu.com for a private online journal site. Each day, or a few times a week, the teacher or a student may provide a prompt or an open-ended question related to the unit or content being studied—or a recent event. In this type of writing, students are not expected to analyze, critique, solve, or summarize. They simply respond to the prompt or the content in any way they choose. For example, a middle school science teacher read aloud a short piece from the news about how honeybees are dying in record numbers. She then asked students what the world would be like without honey bees. Some students took a scientific stance and wrote about the ecological impact, others wrote about their love of honey, others remarked on themes of good riddance because they are allergic to bee stings. It isn't *what* students write for the purpose of this activity, it is *that* they write. The entire process should take no longer than 10 minutes, with five minutes to read text and explain the prompt and five minutes for students to write. Following are tips on content-area journal writing.

1. Students should use the same notebook or online file each day for consistency. Some teachers keep the journals in the classroom and students pick them up as they enter.

2. If students sign up to provide the prompt for specific days, you may want to approve their selection of prompt or content or suggest ideas based on that week's lesson. The prompt should be related to the discipline, if not to the current topic.

3. Students should begin writing when you say "start" and continue writing until you say "stop," usually about five minutes. Ask students not to take think time—they should just begin writing.

4. Facilitate a discussion after the writing session if time allows, or ask the student who provided the prompt to act as discussion facilitator.

5. Don't grade the daily journal writing other than as a completion grade, though you may periodically ask students to revise one of their pieces to turn in for a grade, especially in English classes.

Writing Activity

I don't usually like canned writing activities, but I have had great success in all content areas using RAFT (Role/Audience/Format/Topic), a strategy originally developed by Nancy Vandevanter in 1982. Here's an explanation of the components of RAFT.

Role: What is the writer's role? Who is the writer pretending to be: reporter, observer, eyewitness, object, character in short story, famous person, number, symbol?

Audience: Who will be reading the piece: a character in the story, followers of a blog, the recipient of a letter (a public official, a friend, an object, or animal)?

Format: How will the writer present his piece: letter, speech, blog, tweet, magazine article, news column, travel brochure?

Topic: What is the student writing about?

In social studies or English classes, for example, I often read Eve Bunting's picture book *The Wall* to students as a way of

5.2 Sample RAFT Writing Activities for *The Wall*

Role	Audience	Format	Topic
Little boy	Grandfather	Letter	What he has missed in his life
Father	Vietnam Vets	Blog	His experience with his son
Grandmother	Herself	Journal	How much she misses her husband
The wall	All those who died in the Vietnam War	A newspaper column	What it means to hold the names

building background on the Vietnam Veterans Memorial or the Vietnam War in general. Bunting's book contains a poignant story about a little boy who goes with his father to find his grandfather's name on the wall. When I finish reading, I ask students to choose a RAFT writing activity from Figure 5.2 or make up one of their own. Inevitably, this experience deepens students' understanding of the emotional toll of the Vietnam War in particular and of any war in general.

Figure 5.3 contains sample RAFT writing activities for each content area. Work within your learning community to develop a list of activities for your discipline.

5.3 RAFT Writing Activities in the Content Areas

Content Area	Role	Audience	Format	Topic
Science	tectonic plate	land mass	letter	I can predict your future
Math	variable	equations	song lyrics	You can't live without me
Social Studies	Occupy Wall Street protesters	Martin Luther King Jr.	blog	Tips for nonviolent opposition/resistance
English	comma	student	list	Here's what you need to know about me

Mentor Texts

It is not the role of content-area teachers to teach the craft of writing as English teachers would do, such as developing voice, using dialogue, or writing creatively. Each teacher, however, does have an obligation to show students what proficient writing looks like in her discipline. Writing a line of poetry that employs rhythm or understanding how to use metaphor to clarify ideas is very different from writing to explain the differences among triangles in math, writing about an observation in science, or interpreting a historical account in social studies. Students need to learn how professionals and scholars in various disciplines *use* writing as a tool both to communicate and to further their understanding of the principles and processes in their work. The best way to help students understand how this is done is by providing what is known as mentor texts. Mentor texts, found in all disciplines, are articles, books, and other texts that students can read and analyze as models for their own writing.

Teachers must move away from the textbook to find good content-area writing. As Langer and Applebee point out,

> Textbooks themselves were poor models of writing and thinking within the disciplines they represented. Rather than conveying the excitement of scientific or historical inquiry, the textbooks in those subjects served more as reference guides to scientific or historical information. They were dull and gave little sense of the organizing concepts that might matter within the discipline. (2007, p. 148)

As an example, let's look at an article from *Science Illustrated* "Are Some Volcanoes More Dangerous Than Others?" When using this article with students, I point out that an engaging title, perhaps in the form of a question, goes a long way toward making readers interested in what you have to say. The article begins this way:

> It may seem obvious, but a volcano is only dangerous if there are people living nearby. Antarctica's Mount Erebus

has been erupting continually since 1972 but is harmless since Antarctica is unpopulated. A volcano is otherwise always dangerous if it emits very extensive or explosive eruptions. (2011, p. 22)

I ask students how they might respond as readers to the introductory phrase "It may seem obvious." I also note that the use of a specific example, Antarctica's Mount Erebus, supports the beginning statement and also adds interest.

In contrast, when I look in a middle school science textbook for the same topic, I find only a heading that announces "Volcanoes." The introduction says, "When you think of a volcanic eruption, you might think of a large explosion. However, volcanoes also produce nonexplosive eruptions. The dust, ash, lava, and gas emitted from volcanic eruptions can affect climate and organisms" (McGraw-Hill/Glencoe, 2007, p. 320). This rather choppy paragraph "tells" instead of "shows" and is fairly typical of most textbook writing.

Mentor Texts from Professional Writers

Well-known magazines in a variety of fields employ exemplary writers. Take a look at an article in *Time* by Yale graduate Ishaan Tharoor, a writer-reporter and editor of Global Spin, a foreign affairs blog. He has written extensively on Asian geopolitics. Here is a sentence from one of his articles about Korea's celebration of the Worker's Party: "On Oct. 10, North Korea celebrated 65 years of Workers' party rule—and the anointing of its next leader, Kim Jong Un—with thousands of goose-stepping soldiers marching in concert through the streets of Pyongyang" (Tharoor, 2010, p. 31). The accompanying photograph leaves little doubt about the meaning of "goose-stepping," a perfect adjective to describe the soldiers. To conclude the article, he creatively uses a quote from George Orwell: "Beyond a certain point, military display is only possible in countries where the common people dare not laugh at the army." From this piece of mentor text, high school students can learn how to begin an essay by incorporating facts and still make it creative through the use of a single turn of phrase, "goose-stepping." They can also see how a professional writer chooses to conclude an essay by pulling in the perfect quote.

Mentor texts can be found online, in fiction and nonfiction books, and in news and content-specific magazines such as *Discover, Nature, National Geographic, Smithsonian, Time,* or *Newsweek.* Many of these magazines also have editions for younger students, such as *Time for Kids.* Exposing students to articles that reflect good writing in your discipline helps them become better writers and gives them new information about your topic.

Writing Isn't Always Perfect

Many teachers may relate to the history teacher who told me that she doesn't assign much writing because she's afraid she won't catch every mistake. It's no secret that even some English teachers don't know every grammatical rule in the book, some math and social studies teachers can't identify prepositional phrases, and some science teachers have written so many lab notes in phrases that they think fragments *are* sentences. That's the nature of content-area writing.

Some educators fall into the trap of creating a schoolwide writing plan that emphasizes correctness at the expense of learning. Content-area writing is all about content, not about grammar, not about complete paragraphs with topic and concluding sentences, and not about infallible correctness. Although most educators want to support the notion of grammatically correct writing, the most important goal is to have students learn to use writing as a tool for thinking. As the National Commission on Writing points out, "Writing extends far beyond mastering grammar and punctuation. The ability to diagram a sentence does not make a good writer. There are many students capable of identifying every part of speech who are barely able to produce a piece of prose" (2003, p. 13). Writing is learning, and learning rarely happens without error. At some point, usually in the final draft of a formal paper, students will be expected to use standard grammar and punctuation, but initially they must be free from the constraints of grammar to think through ideas and concepts while writing to learn.

Writing to learn also doesn't mean writing to a formula, writing five-paragraph essays, or writing a pristine paper. As Langer and Applebee caution,

> If writing is to play a meaningful role in subjects other than English, then the teachers of those subjects will need to have a conception of writing specific to their disciplines, one that emphasizes what is unique about writing (and thinking) in their subject, rather than one that emphasizes ways in which such activities will foster the work of the English teachers. (2007, p. 150)

Providing Feedback

If content-area teachers aren't expected to grade students' papers for grammar, how do you help students write effective pieces? If your role is to help students learn in your discipline, and writing is a literacy tool that makes that happen, it allows you to see composition in a new light. Just as you want your students to become independent readers who can access content, you want them to become independent writers as well. Think of yourself as a coach who prompts students to deepen their thinking, organize their ideas, and effectively communicate what they want to say.

Read through student papers or notebooks and merely provide feedback in the form of responses, such as the following:

- You almost have it! Try . . .
- I like the way you're thinking here. Now, have you considered . . .
- What do you think should come next here?
- This idea is confusing. Could you explain further?
- Yes! That's it! Good thinking!
- Consider what would happen if . . .
- Have you forgotten about [this aspect] of the argument?

Remember that you don't have to respond to everything students write, just as you don't have to grade everything they write. In fact, students can take some of the load off of you by learning to respond to their peers' writing if they are given time to practice. Such critical reading and responding to peer writing is an authentic way to learn what works (and what doesn't) in a piece. If you must keep daily grades, consider completion scores instead of assigning a numerical grade to each piece of writing.

Digital Writing

In response to schools adopting digital textbooks and students being fluent in digital communication we should also adapt schoolwork to digital writing. For example, many high school English and social studies teachers are entering the national discussion about replacing traditional research papers with new literacies such as blogs, tweets, and multimedia presentations. Dr. Lunsford, a professor of English at Stanford, has been studying how students' writing abilities and passions are changing as multimedia tools are entering classrooms and concluded that when students use such tools they are actually producing something "rewarding and valuable, whereas when they write a term paper, they feel as if they do so only to produce a grade" (Richtel, 2012, p. 3). Once you begin to incorporate technology into your writing instruction, you will find advantages in the form of students' engagement, increased collaboration, and deeper understanding of the content.

Blogs

A blog is an online collection of commentary and links that can be used to facilitate open discussions in any class. As Troy Hicks notes, "The goal is for students to create their own blogs and connect their ideas to those of their peers" (2009, p. 39). Hicks suggests that students create blogs through a free service such as Edublogs (www.edublogs.org) or Class Blogmeister (www.classblogmeister.com) or by creating a social network with built-in blogging through Ning (www.ning.com). The advantages of blogs are that students can read and respond to the blogs of others, thus creating an online discussion that helps them synthesize ideas and use writing as a tool for communicating. Coupled with rich content, blogging increases collaborative possibilities for students and teachers. For example, an 8th grade English teacher works with a social studies teacher on a Holocaust unit in which each student is assigned the name of a real person who lived during this period. As students do research about the time period, they will create blogs as if they were the person they have been assigned and write about their experiences. As the unit progresses, they will respond to other students' blogs and learn to hyperlink to sources of information about the country in which their person lived. Blogging has the potential to turn any assignment into an interactive experience that goes beyond a bland textbook account of this horrible period in history.

English teachers are especially enamored with blogs because they are perfect tools for teaching peer revision. Students can write privately, just as they do with paper and pen, and then post their work to the public portion of their blog for peer feedback. "Showing students how you post your own writing and modeling the kind of response that you want them to give to one another should help alleviate their fears of sharing digital writing, just as it would in traditional writing practices" (Hicks, 2009, p. 42).

Wikis

A wiki is a website that is all about sharing information, so it is a great tool for small groups or an entire class and also includes a discussion forum. The best example of a wiki is Wikipedia, which students are sure to know. Use it as a model when showing students how their wikis could look and how projects can develop over time instead of having a definite starting and ending point. A 5th grade social studies teacher created a wiki for the ubiquitous state assignment, for which each student chooses a state to research. Instead of the traditional oral report along with a visual aid, her students posted their findings on a wiki. Since wikis encourage collaborative writing, a practice also recommended by the *Writing Next* report (Graham & Perin, 2007), students were able to revise each other's reports if they knew something about a state, perhaps from background knowledge, that was not in the original report.

Before getting your students started with wikis, take a look at the user-friendly Wikispaces (www.wikispaces.com) and be sure to read teacher tips for wiki projects at http://digitallyspeaking.pbworks.com/f/Handout_TeacherTipsWikiProjects.pdf.

Google Docs

Consider having students use Google Docs (https://docs.google.com) when writing, especially for English class. Google Docs is a free Internet site that uses a document drafting program that will look familiar to most of us and also offers useful tools that allow students to create spreadsheets, forms, and presentations. The advantage is that students can upload, access, and share documents from any computer. What's more, this tool makes it easy not only for the teacher to offer feedback in a variety of ways, but peer revision is also easy.

Becoming a Content-Area Teacher of Writing

For a teacher who has not been trained in writing, the idea of meeting the high demands of the Common Core State Standards in writing can be a bit formidable. Even if you feel you don't have the skills necessary to become a content-area teacher of writing, or if you don't see yourself as a great writer, you can become a good writing teacher. The place to start is simply giving students many opportunities to write in a variety of ways.

Figure 5.4 will help you reflect on your role as a content-area teacher who sees writing as a springboard for learning. Use the questions to prompt your thinking about how you can help students become first-rate writers in your discipline.

Writing: A Valuable Tool for Learning

The National Commission on Writing advises that "The valuable tool of writing must be put back in the hands of schoolteachers,

5.4 How to Create Writers in Content-Area Classes

- Provide daily opportunities for students to write.
- Ask students to analyze instead of to merely summarize.
- Give students opportunities for self-reflection and sufficient time to work through the messy process of discovery and inquiry through writing.
- Model how people in your field write.
- Deemphasize note-taking and encourage analytical writing and deeper reasoning.
- Allow students to collaborate when writing.
- Allow students choice in their writing.
- Ask students to write for authentic audiences.
- Encourage students to use digital writing tools, especially for collaborative writing.
- Emphasize the content of what students write rather than the correctness of what they write.
- Relax and enjoy your role as a supporter, rather than acting as an evaluator.

not because writing is an optional talent that students might find useful at some point in their lives, but because writing (and the conceptual skills it reflects and develops) opens up new and powerful means of learning for all students" (2006, p. 16). Content-area teachers can take advantage of this literacy tool to help their students deeply understand the concepts that often elude them when reading the textbook. Even a few minutes of writing in every class, every day, will provide your students with an advantage that will immeasurably support them in their academic endeavors for the rest of their lives.

Community of Practice: Writing to Learn

In this Community of Practice, you will support each other in creating, teaching, and evaluating write-to-learn lessons. Following is a suggested outline for your group's activities.

In the meeting

1. In content-area groups, talk about the next chapter or unit you plan to teach, even if teachers from different grade levels will teach different units.
2. Help each other develop at least one write-to-learn assignment based on the topic.

3. Spend a few minutes writing and brainstorming about the assignment. For example, address why this particular assignment is relevant to students' learning, what your students should expect to learn from this assignment, and how you will introduce and monitor the assignment. You will be better able to help students in their writing if you are a writer yourself.

In the classroom

4. Each teacher presents a lesson with the writing assignment in at least one class. If possible, work with a peer teacher who can be in the room during the lesson to observe the process and interact with students. (An ideal situation would be co-teaching as explained in Appendix D.) Both of you should observe and take notes about the points noted in step 5.

In the follow-up meeting

5. At the next meeting, take turns discussing the assignment.

- How did students respond to the assignment?
- What did you learn about your students' success or difficulty with the topic of study?
- What suggestions do others in the group have about revising the assignment?
- How did you feel about not grading the assignment but merely responding to it?
- Each member should read at least one student paper to the group and ask how they would respond to the student regarding his piece.

6. Help each other create write-to-learn assignments for the next chapter or unit.

7. If time permits, discuss how your students could use an interactive notebook, learning log, or journal across the grade levels in your discipline. Have a group member keep notes and readdress the topic at the next meeting until everyone has a plan for incorporating these tools into lessons for your discipline.

8. Choose a book on writing and begin a book study if your group does not feel comfortable as teachers of writing in your discipline. See Appendix A, Book Study Essentials, for information on creating an effective book study. Books that specifically address writing in disciplines include the following:

- *But How Do You Teach Writing? A Simple Guide for All Teachers* by B. Lane
- *Content-Area Writing: Every Teacher's Guide* by H. Daniels, S. Zemelman, and N. Steineke
- *Teaching Science with Interactive Notebooks* by K. Marcarelli
- *Write Like This: Teaching Real-World Writing Through Modeling and Mentor Texts* by K. Gallagher
- *Writing in Science in Action: Strategies, Tools, and Classroom Video* by B. R. Fulwiler

6

Assessing for Learning

When I first started teaching, assessment was a matter of giving a test, grading it, going over it with your students, and moving on to the next topic. Now, we know so much more about assessment that it has taken on a language of its own: formative, summative, standardized, performance, standards-based. And there is a whole vocabulary associated with it: proficiency, AYP, rubric, high-stakes. We have assessments that drive instruction, assessments that determine your students' futures, and assessments that wake you up in the middle of the night. A PLC or community of practice session on assessment might well turn into a counseling session.

Unfortunately, it is with assessment that textbooks have failed us more than in any other area. Oh, there are plenty of assessments in textbooks; in fact, most come with whole sections of assessments and many provide separate booklets or CDs of assessments, but it is impossible for textbooks to take the place of teachers working together as they do in high-performing schools to develop assessments based on what they know about their students and the topic of study.

Compare textbook assessments that unapologetically offer standardized test preparation in the form of multiple-choice or short-answer items with Linda Darling-Hammond's description of assessments in successful schools:

> Most assignments require the production of analytic work—research papers and projects, demonstrations and discussions of problems, experiments and data collection organized to answer open-ended questions. Worksheets and fill-in-the-blank tasks are rare. Extensive reading and writing are expected in all academic courses. Many classes require large end-of-course projects that include extensive written documentation, often presented and defended orally. (2010a, pp. 250–251)

Many textbook publishers are making an effort to move toward more meaningful assessments, such as with this prompt in a 5th grade elementary social studies textbook, "Select a country in Europe and imagine you live there. Write a letter to your friend in America explaining why you think he or she should visit this country." Although this is an improvement over fill-in-the-blank assessments, it still has a long way to go to be effective. The problem is that textbook assessments generally are generic, set-in-stone questions or tasks that are to be assigned to all students, no matter where or how they live. Teachers, not textbooks, have the unique ability to truly evaluate students' grasp of content.

Teaching to the Test: The Failed Practice of Ubiquitous Test Prep

I will not rant about the evils of how standardized test scores are used in most of the United States to rank, sort, and penalize students, teachers, and schools, but I will note that such an approach is the exact opposite of how high-achieving nations use assessments. In Finland, for example, the state-mandated testing system used to track students has been eliminated, and assessments are focused on "problem solving, creativity, independent learning and student reflection" (Darling-Hammond, 2010a, p 5). Top-performing nations are increasingly relying on assessments that include research projects, investigation, and other intellectually challenging work—developed and scored by teachers. Although individual schools and districts cannot change the testing frenzy mandated by their state and the federal government, they can be smart about how they approach it—and substituting test prep for assessments that inform instruction simply isn't smart.

The ills of creating a curriculum around test prep are numerous and well-known, including narrowing the curriculum to only topics that are tested, but here are two of the most significant reasons to refuse to buy (or buy into) test prep materials:

Teaching to the test has a dumbing-down effect on both teaching and learning. The more teachers provide worksheets, drills, practice tests, and other techniques for memorizing facts rather than understanding content (even during the first or last ten minutes of class), the less students tap into higher-order thinking skills (Volante, 2004). In fact, there is research that shows that students have become adept at scanning a text to find an answer to a question and responding to it correctly without demonstrating any understanding of the content (Neil, 2003). Combine that with students having no ownership over their own learning, and what we have created, however inadvertently, is a *nonthinking* curriculum.

A focus on improving only standardized test scores with its accompanying competition, anxiety, and scripted teaching is detrimental to whole-school cohesion as well as to individual teachers, many of whom are throwing in the towel and leaving the profession for good. Such an atmosphere results in teachers who feel disempowered and unmotivated. As one award-winning middle-school teacher whose district uses a prescriptive program told me, "It's all about test scores. I used to enjoy teaching and my students enjoyed coming to school. They loved to read, write, and do projects. Now, the district *says* they want innovative teaching, but it's like I have cinderblocks on my feet because they really only want me to follow a program designed to raise test scores."

The practice of following a prescriptive program, prevalent in many districts that I visit, is counterproductive to the goals of school systems and state departments of education. Undeniably, what they want is increased student achievement, but a unilateral focus on test scores derails initiatives where teachers work together to assess students for the purpose of improving teaching and learning. In fact, research on teacher uncertainty (low sense of efficacy and self-esteem) has been tied to *decreased* student achievement (Fullan, 2007). So, we must reclaim assessment in our own classrooms and turn it into what it was intended to be, a tool that informs our instruction.

The Purpose of Assessment

I found a great definition of assessment in a book with the delightful title *A Pig Don't Get Fatter the More You Weigh It: Classroom Assessments That Work.* "The purpose of using any form of assessment is to provide clarity about the learner's strengths and to inform the teacher about any area of growth that may need attention. Assessment not only provides an understanding of the learner's needs, it is also informing the teachers about how their instruction and their curriculum are evolving" (Rushton & Juola-Rushton, 2007, p. 30). The key point in this definition is that assessment should be used to help teachers make decisions about how to revise their teaching and where to go next with instruction. In the past, we assessed for the purpose of obtaining a grade to report on students' progress, usually with parents as the intended audience. Often, behavior and participation were also factors in grades. Now we understand how important it is to use assessment as a tool for helping students become better learners. Richard Stiggins asks two important questions:

- How can we use assessment to help all our students *want* to learn?
- How can we help them feel *able* to learn? (2002, p. 758)

In looking at textbook assessments, few of them address these questions. Instead, the items are generally grouped at the end of the chapter in categories such as "Review," "Recall," "Understand," "Think Critically," and "Apply." Although these headings make sense in terms of models such as Bloom's taxonomy or Webb's depth of knowledge, they fall short in connecting students to the excitement of new learning. Instead of giving students opportunities to show what they know or to demonstrate how learning new information has made a difference in their thinking, many textbook questions revert to the 20th century practice of posing a question with one expected and correct answer to find out if students have read the chapter.

The popular metaphor of using assessment to drive instruction makes me think of cowboys driving cattle across the range, whips snapping, dogs nipping, horses raising dust around the herd. Publishers follow the national education trends, and under No Child Left Behind that trend didn't make students (or teachers) think of assessment as something positive. We are seeing signs that the federal government is removing some of the barbs from testing, but that remains to be seen.

Checking for Understanding

Doug Fisher and Nancy Frey's term, also the title of their book on assessment, *Checking for Understanding,* has a much more positive (and accurate) take on assessment. They talk about assessment as a method that corrects misconceptions while improving learning. In my work with teachers, I find that those who continually check for understanding have more engaged students *and* higher test scores. I observed a 4th grade math teacher who rarely used textbook assessments. Instead, she taught students to raise their hands at any point when they were confused or didn't "get" the idea or lesson and she went straight to them. Her class was arranged in small groups, and she often moved students around so they could benefit from their peers. The community in that class was not one of competition because grades were rarely mentioned. It was a place where everyone shared knowledge and helped each other in understanding. By the way, this teacher was also gifted in explaining and assessing concepts in various ways: art, hands-on manipulatives, foldables, writing, and stories using numbers as characters. Creative assessments often decorated the walls in her classroom as well as the halls outside her class. Students enjoyed multiple forms of assessment and they continued learning as she checked for their understanding.

The buzzword for such ongoing checking for understanding is *formative assessment,* as opposed to *summative assessment,* which is assessment used at the end of a unit or grading period. Formative assessment is a critical element in creating successful schools. Mike Schmoker, an author who has written extensively on school improvement, notes, "Thanks to the British educator Dylan Wiliam and others, we now know that the consistent delivery of lessons that include multiple checks for understanding may be the most powerful, cost-effective action we can take to ensure learning. Solid research demonstrates that students learn as much as four times as quickly from such lessons" (Schmoker, 2010, p. 23).

What Does It Mean to Understand?

Before we assess for learning, it is important to spend some time thinking (and discussing) what we mean when we say that students "understand" a concept. In *Understanding by Design,* Grant Wiggins and Jay McTighe discuss the concept of understanding and describe it as "more than just textbook knowledge and skill." When students really "get it," they have "sophisticated insights and abilities, reflected in varied performances and contexts" (1998, p. 5). Significantly, the authors note, "Knowing the facts and doing well on tests of knowledge does not mean that we understand" (1998, p. 39). It's clear that assessing for understanding is more than "teaching to the test" or casually monitoring learning; it is a process that changes with each topic, each class, and each individual student.

Unfortunately, there are few surefire strategies for assessing understanding. Teachers need to be watchful for signs of learning as well as for signs of confusion. Many teachers do this informally, such as asking students for a show of hands (or thumbs up, thumbs down signs) during a discussion or lesson, carefully listening to a small group discussion, or having students fill out an exit slip. The teacher turns into a keen observer of student behavior and student work. One of the reasons that co-teaching or peer coaching is so effective is that there is another set of eyes and ears to evaluate whether students are understanding the lesson. Equally important is the dialogue with another teacher about activities or instruction that will help those who are having difficulty.

Evidence of Understanding

Even if you are as vigilant as a dog under the dinner table waiting for crumbs to drop, it is not always so easy to determine if students *really* know or if they are pretending to know. Students have been conditioned to figure out the answer that the teacher wants—and have become pretty good at providing just that—without full understanding. Many textbook assessments contribute to this problem. In a 7th grade science textbook, I found this assessment: "List the four processes in the formation of sedimentary rocks." Students may list "weathering, transportation, deposition, and lithification" and get full credit for their answer, or they may list "weathering and transportation," which gets them half credit. What does the answer to that question provide to the teachers? Not much if they are looking for evidence of understanding.

Compare that assessment to this one: "Turn to your learning partner and describe how rocks weather. Then, change partners and describe how rocks are transported." The teacher instructs students to engage in this activity for each of the processes as she walks around the classroom listening to descriptions and correcting faulty understandings. She may then ask the class at the end of the activity if anyone still doesn't understand any of the processes. In an environment where learning, not evaluating, is the focus, students are much more likely to come clean and say they don't get it—or to ask questions to clarify their understanding.

Criteria for Evaluating Textbook Assessments

Just as I advocate using textbooks as only one of many resources for curriculum, I also suggest that we should be using them as resources for assessments. With your learning community, look through the many assessments offered in your teacher editions and find those that can be used or adapted in a meaningful way for your unit of study. When assessing students, it helps to know in your own mind what you mean by understanding the content. What is it you expect of students? How will you make sure that they have met your expectations? What are the criteria for a good textbook assessment? Use the questions below to aid you in your search or as you create new assessments.

- Does the assessment align with your teaching goals? It doesn't matter how creative or engaging the assessment is if it doesn't provide evidence of specific learning.
- Does the assessment demonstrate students' understanding rather than requiring simple memorization or finding an answer in the text? Can students make inferences, interpret information, or use what they have learned in new settings?
- Does the assessment allow for flexibility in the way students respond, such as through discussion, demonstration, or performance?
- Does the assessment ask that students use their learning as evidence to justify a position, solve a problem, or extend learning?

Ongoing, Embedded Assessment

Many teachers use the age-old pop quiz as a type of formative assessment. Pop quizzes do provide information to the teacher quickly, but the quality of the information is often unreliable. Students may have forgotten what they have read, know the answers to other questions about the topic but not to the few questions that the teacher has chosen to ask, or may be able to provide a superficial answer that allows them to pass the test without in-depth comprehension. Following are other ways to incorporate ongoing assessment into any unit or textbook chapter.

Responses

In a classroom focused on learning, students should expect the question "What do you think?" at any time during the period and be ready to respond. Learning logs, described in Chapter 5, are good places to have students record answers to this question. Teachers can read the answers quickly, especially when they are concerned about a particular student, and get a good idea of the student's understanding.

Another way students can respond is through an adaptation of the Think-Pair-Share strategy described in Chapter 1, which is great for making sure all students are involved in the discussion. In pairs, students take turns telling each other about the topic. After the partners share their thoughts, they collaborate to write a sentence summarizing their discussion. Each team then reads the sentence to the class.

With a mathematical problem, for example, you might ask students what they think is the best way to set up the problem to find a solution. In science, they might respond to a question about why they think the lab experiment turned out the way it did. In English, the responses are unlimited: Why do you think the character behaves the way he does? What do you think about the way the poet uses a certain line? In social studies this activity provides an opportunity for students to go beyond parroting facts from the text. Ask them, for instance, to turn to a partner and talk about why they think black soldiers fought on the side of the Confederacy.

Student-Teacher Conferences

In classrooms where students are actively working together, there is time for the teacher to sit down beside students and conduct informal assessments. If kids are silently reading a short story in English language arts, for example, the teacher may go from student to student and quietly ask if there is anything they don't understand or even ask them to summarize what they have read to determine if they are comprehending the text. Mini-conferences can be scheduled periodically when students are working on a paper or a project, with more time given to those who most need it.

Teachers who keep folders (electronic or on paper) about each student can make brief notes during these meetings about students' learning needs and refer back to them at the next conference to track growth. Many English teachers use conferences to read through student writing and make suggestions or monitor a skill that a particular student may have been working on, such as organization or transitions. Conferences can be used by teachers in every discipline as an effective formative assessment.

Oral Assessments

Ben Dykema was a teacher who loved to use oral assessments in his 9th grade government class. Students sat in a large circle as he initiated discussions based on the topic of study. Students not only answered Mr. Dykema's questions, but they also responded to classmates' comments. He kept a clipboard on the desk and made notes about students' understandings beside their names. Mr. Dykema didn't ask low-level questions. I remember that he once asked a student why she would vote for a particular candidate since she saw herself as a fiscal conservative. Mr. Dykema prompted students to use their newly learned knowledge and could readily see which students had trouble understanding. On more than one occasion, Mr. Dykema went back to the original lesson and retaught the concepts in a different way after listening to a student discussion. It is telling that when he taught AP/U.S. government, a higher percentage of his students passed the AP test than students of the other advanced placement teachers in the school.

Demonstrations

Linda Darling-Hammond talks about assessments in high-achieving countries: "Their assessments, most of which are open-ended performance assessments, require students to demonstrate what they can do with what they are learning" (2010b, p. 35). Especially in math and science, ask students to show what they know. They can do this in small groups or with learning partners. In a classroom community where everyone understands that each of us has different strengths and challenges, students will not feel diminished if Sierra works with LaShaun because he can demonstrate the relationship between a percent and a decimal in math to her, and she can then demonstrate her knowledge to you.

Another way of demonstrating knowledge is through drawings. Provide unlined paper and markers—even high school students respond positively to this hands-on task. Ask them to draw how a lever works in science, for example, or to create a symbol that represents how the character in a short story feels after a significant event.

In one middle-school English class, I asked students to respond in writing to a short story about prejudice. One young man immediately began sketching a heart surrounded by unsheathed swords. My first impulse as the quintessential teacher was to remind him that he was to *write,* but, fortunately, I came to my senses and asked him how his sketch symbolized prejudice. Soon, the rest of the class gathered around as he talked about his experience with prejudice and the pain it caused him. He did end up writing after all, but he needed to demonstrate his understanding of the story first by drawing; I may never have known just how much he understood if I had insisted that he write a paragraph, or worse, answer a fill-in-the-blank question.

Summative Assessments

Summative assessments are assessments *of* learning (rather than *for* learning) that are given at the end of the unit or grading period and are used to determine what students know. Traditionally, these tests have been pen and paper tests—sometimes even in subjects such as music, speech, and drama. If this is the case in your school or district, I suggest that you use your learning community to make a strong case for performance assessments, assessments that show not only what students know but what they can do, in addition to written exams.

Portfolios

A portfolio is a collection of items that is assembled by students or their teachers to show a range of work in a subject. Art teachers are familiar with this tool, as are English teachers who keep students' writing in one designated place. Portfolios are a great way to assess students in both formative and summative ways. Students can learn to take ownership of their portfolios and use them to showcase work that they feel demonstrates their knowledge and abilities. Instead of the snapshot view that many tests provide, portfolios show a continuum of learning. What's more, students take pride in their portfolios and often go beyond the basic requirements. The same student who wads up a test and arcs it into the nearest wastebasket can be caught redoing portfolio work to show his achievements. For teachers, this tool provides a range of student learning for assessment.

For a structured portfolio, you can provide the activities and assignments for each student's portfolio, and students will create a table of contents that reflects their work. Note, too, that digital portfolios are highly engaging and allow students to experiment with technology. Portfolios can be presented through a website or slide show. According to Troy Hicks, blogfolios, blogs that are transformed into a digital portfolio, "create a unique opportunity for a digital writer to make a personalized portfolio" (2009, p. 84).

When the portfolio is complete, based on a prearranged deadline, the teacher and student sit down together, review the portfolio, and then come to an agreement about the final grade the student has earned. In my experience, students are either on the mark with the grade or they score themselves lower than I would. Discussing and grading the portfolio with your students helps them assume responsibility; they quickly come to realize that the work they are doing is not for me but for themselves. It is their portfolio, not mine.

Example of a Science Portfolio. A portfolio on genetics in a 5th or 8th grade science class includes assignments that have been discussed several times throughout the unit, with the teacher modeling and giving students feedback as they work. Feedback may be in written form or it may be oral, such as during a student conference. The difference between a traditional assessment and this performance assessment is that each item is not graded immediately upon its completion. The items are collected in a portfolio and the final grade given once the portfolio is in order. Of course, there would be a designated ending date, but students who polish their portfolios early may turn them in early.

Following are examples of items that may be required for a science portfolio on genetics.

1. Web quest based on one of the following essential questions.

    - Why is Mendel's work important?
    - What is a genetic disorder?
    - What is genetic engineering?

    Note: Include lists of resources, interview notes, Internet findings, and rough drafts of the final piece.

2. Persuasion paper on why genetically modified plants are a positive or negative contribution to society.

    Note: Include rough drafts, peer reviewers' notes, and research used to form a conclusion.

3. Reflection piece about what you learned during the lab on probability.

4. A graphic organizer that shows your understanding of the differences between phenotype and genotype.
5. Illustration of Mendel's pea traits.

Performance Assessments

As mentioned in the chapter on engagement, students have more investment in their learning when they have a degree of choice and control. Offering students the option of doing a project rather than taking a test has the distinct advantage of allowing students to engage in learning while demonstrating knowledge. Linda Darling-Hammond reports on several hundred new schools in New York City that are "graduating students at twice the rate of the factory-model warehouses they replaced" (2010a, p. 235). What is their secret? Students engage in project-based learning and performance assessments. Sometimes students submit a portfolio that is similar (but more in-depth) to that described in the previous section. It would include "high-quality work illustrating disciplinary inquiry in each of the major subject areas" (Darling-Hammond, 2010a, p. 257).

Sample Textbook Performance Assessments

Many textbooks have sections that target real world learning. For example, in a high school science textbook, the editors suggest having students create a sketch of a flower garden for a certain plot of ground. Students are asked to research which plants would flourish best in the garden site of their choice. Such prompts could be extended to having students take photographs of areas around their neighborhoods and design flower gardens, perhaps even asking the owners if they can take a soil sample so they know what would grow best and then showing them their designs at the end of the project. A 10th grade science/math interdisciplinary team collaborated on a composting project where math students figured out the dimensions of the composting site as well as ratios of types of compostable materials; science students worked to create the compost and explained to visitors how to make their own. A middle school English teacher asked students to provide to their groups lyrics of songs that included at least three examples of figurative language instead of giving a pen and paper test on poetry.

Other performance-based assessments that you may find suggested in your textbook include

- Project exhibits
- Oral presentations
- Debates
- Panel discussions on open-ended questions
- Lab experiments
- Multimedia presentations
- Demonstrations of experiments or solutions to problems
- Reader's theater, skits, plays, speeches
- Interviews
- Visual displays: graphs, charts, posters, illustrations, storyboards, cartoons
- Photo essays
- Models
- Blogs, wikis, or other electronic projects

Assessing New Literacies

Consider new literacies in looking at assessments as well, such as critical, visual, and digital literacy, especially as you work outside the textbook. Critical literacy requires that students recognize literacy as a tool for social action, "understanding the ways in which language and literacy are used to accomplish social ends" (Dozier, Johnston, & Rogers, 2006, p. 18). Look for assessments through which students can demonstrate that they know

- The author's intents and motives.
- Whose perspective has been left out.
- If the author is biased.
- If the source is reliable.
- Whose values are represented.

Visual literacy is simply the ability to interpret and make meaning from images. Although textbooks are full of images, few assessments target the important skill of *reading* visual text. Use these questions to create assessments or to evaluate those in the textbook.

- What message does the image send?
- Who is sending the message?
- What has been left out of the image, graph, or illustration?
- How does the image manipulate the reader's feelings or intellect?
- What is the significance of the image?
- Is the source or image itself legitimate?

Assess students' competence with digital literacy within your discipline just as you would assess their ability to use any tool critical to understanding the content. Look for assessments that indicate students' ability to

- Effectively synthesize multiple sources of information.
- Compare and contrast sites.
- Determine the reliability of the site.
- Communicate effectively with the tools of technology.
- Find and use valid information to research a topic.

Self-Assessment

If you have ever taken a yoga class (or played any sport), you know the advantages of self-assessment. The teacher can coach you by reminding you to distribute your weight between the front and back of your feet, for example, but only *you* know if that is really happening. Often my yoga instructor will tell the class to look at a place on our bodies, such as our hands, to *self-assess* our progress. Similarly, in classroom learning, "Self-assessment by pupils, far from being a luxury, is in fact *an essential component of formative assessment*" (Black & Wiliam, 1998, p. 143). Just as I become more confident in my yogic abilities when I see my foot positioned the right way or realize that I have finally learned how to balance in a particular pose, students develop confidence as learners when they experience success. They then are encouraged to take additional academic risks, which is especially important for students who have been labeled low-achieving (Stiggins, 2002).

How can we incorporate self-assessment in our classroom practice? First, we must learn to give over some of our control to students and allow them to discover for themselves their individual learning poses. Unfortunately, textbooks fail us in this area of assessment as well. The textbook, by its very nature, is a tool of authority—it presents the facts as well as the assessments from the perspective of the all-knowing. Not only do students rarely question what they read unless we have taught them about critical literacy, but they are rarely asked to think about their learning. Sadly, there is often little need to self-assess because the instructions are usually quite clear: list, describe, take notes, explain, determine, infer, write. The correct answers are printed definitively in the teacher's edition.

Imagine that for every assignment, students were taught to look back over their learning and to determine for themselves if they really got it. If they discover that they don't fully understand, however, they must be free to redo the assignment or a portion of it so they can build their sense of self-efficacy, the belief and determination that they can succeed. Just as I encourage the use of a self-reflection sheet for writing, I also advocate that teachers provide a place in the learning log for student self-evaluation.

Equally important is having students set specific learning goals, a component of engagement. Students can then monitor their understanding and decide for themselves if they have reached their goals—or are on their way. They can also come to understand *why* they are having difficulty and to discover how to realign their learning, a strategy that will serve them well for life.

Let's consider a lesson from a 5th grade textbook on life in the southern colonies. The teacher and students together develop the goal for studying this time period, perhaps to understand the difference between life on large plantations and life on small farms. As students read, discuss, and organize their notes about the differences, the teacher will be looking for a lack of understanding, and the students *as well* will be aware of gaps in their knowledge. It will take a while to move this responsibility to students, but it can be accomplished by incorporating mechanisms for students to practice metacognition, the ability to monitor their own learning. The following prompts and questions will help students with this process.

- My goal for this chapter, topic, or unit:
- The most important thing I learned from the text, assignment, or project:
- I still don't understand:
- This part of the lesson/text/assignment was difficult for me:
- What I learned will help me in this way:
- After doing this assignment or reading this text, I now see this in a different way:
- I feel I have/have not met my goal for learning this topic because:
- This part of the assignment was really hard because:
- I would like to redo part of the assignment in this way:

Redos

In our obsession with grades carved in stone and the negative connotation we have attached to the word *failure,* we sometimes forget just how much we learn from making mistakes. Unfortunately, textbook publishers rarely consider the value of error when they offer assessments. Their assessments are one-time shots because they have not built in time for the *process* of learning. This is, perhaps, my greatest criticism of using textbooks as a curriculum guide. We must look at the learner, not merely at what is to be learned, and allow students to try and try again if that's what it takes for them to understand.

Brian Cambourne's famous model of learning includes what he calls "approximation," or "having a go at it." He says "Freedom to approximate is an essential ingredient of all successful learning" (1988, p. 70). One of the best ways to encourage students to learn from their mistakes is to allow them to redo their work.

Rick Wormeli, in an article titled "Redos and Retakes Done Right," makes this point beautifully.

> LSAT. MCAT. Praxis, SAT. Bar exam. CPA exam. Driver's lisensure. Pilot's licensure. Auto mechanic certification exam. Every one of these assessments reflects the adult-level working-world responsibilities our students will one day face. Many of them are high stakes: People's lives depend on these tests' validity as accurate measures of individual competence. All of them can be redone over and over *for full credit.* (2011, p. 24)

It is time to move from an unrealistic system where students have only one chance to get it right to a system where they understand that redos are not only OK but expected. It is ironic that with all of the national rhetoric from politicians and educational leaders about how to increase the graduation rate, close the achievement gap, and make our students competitive with those from high-achieving nations, we rarely hear anything about the process of learning. Like the scientific method itself, learning is a type of hypothesis testing: making an educated guess, learning from that guess, and redoing the "experiment" with new knowledge.

How to Manage Redos

I encourage teachers to allow students to redo work, but I am aware that such a policy runs the risk of making them crazy. When sanity is at stake, always err on the side of stability, but give redos a try before making a decision. Following are some tips for keeping redos from becoming a logistical nightmare.

- Have students explain in writing why they want the opportunity for a redo and submit their previous attempt along with the request.
- When students submit the redo, have them highlight the revised part of the assessment and answer the question, How does this revised assessment show evidence of increased learning?
- For subjects such as math or science, give a different, more challenging problem if appropriate. In English or social studies, you may ask students to complete a redo on a different piece of text.
- You don't have to read each step of the redo as the student makes improvements. You might simply need to be available for a conference to offer brief feedback.
- Encourage peer or self-assessment of the redo until the student feels the assignment is ready to be turned in for a grade.
- When reevaluating, look only at the revised part of the assignment; don't feel compelled to read the entire assessment again.
- Have students place redos in a separate basket and tell them that you will reassess when you get to it.
- Deemphasize grades in favor of increased learning. Students should expect that you will not hurry to change a grade on a report card. Wait until you have several new grades to change and do them all at once—at your convenience.
- It is your prerogative to put students who abuse the redo privilege on probation.
- Set reasonable deadlines for redos according to your schedule and time constraints.
- Remember that the goal of having students redo assignments is to engage them in deeper learning, not grade swapping.

Daniel Pink talks about a famous experiment where scientists placed puzzles in monkeys' cages to test their ability to solve the puzzles. Suddenly, the monkeys began "playing with the puzzles with focus, determination and what looked like enjoyment" (2011, p. 2). Pink's point is that nobody rewarded them with anything—not praise, food, affection, *nor grades*. The scientists determined that the primates were engaged in intrinsic rewards, the joy of the task being its own reward. That is the basic premise of redos, that students become interested in a task or assessment because the drive to discover, solve, and succeed trumps the desire to gain a grade or your approval. The more your class resembles a learning lab where students work on authentic, relevant projects and research—and are allowed the advantage of self-reflection—the more students will become independent in their quest for knowledge. Assessment will simply become a by-product of the entire process.

Learners as Apprentices

The apprentice method of learning is not such a bad idea. When a carpenter wanted to learn the trade, he followed a master who was skilled in that trade until becoming a master himself. What we know of learning now follows that model pretty closely. Learning must be demonstrated by one who is adept at what is to be learned, and the learner is expected to practice, ask questions, take responsibility, and listen to the feedback given by the teacher.

Teacher feedback should be ongoing, often in response to questions from the learner, and sometimes as the teacher sees the learner making a mistake. Cambourne further describes feedback by saying that it should be readily available, nonthreatening, and with no strings attached; in addition, there should not be a penalty for not getting the learning correct the next time it is produced (Cambourne, 1988).

Feedback is at the core of learning, as Socrates knew, as countless apprentices knew, and as any of us who have had children know. And that component of assessment is something that corporate test makers simply can't do, no matter how much we pay them.

The Power of Assessment

Assessment, whether formative or summative, has the power to motivate students to take pride in their achievements or to view learning as an external product that belongs to someone, anyone, other than themselves. In schools where learning is perceived as a challenging and exciting process, assessment is an integral part of the entire educational experience. In schools where test scores trump every other aspect of schooling, assessment is a fear-driven exercise that diminishes the inherent joy in learning and actually has a negative impact on the outcome. Although we have less control over assessment than we might like, we can still make the evaluation process a meaningful and positive experience in all disciplines.

Community of Practice: Assessing for Learning

In this Community of Practice activity, your group will read about and discuss all facets of assessment in order to lay the groundwork for developing and using effective assessments.

Before the meeting

1. Assessment for learning deserves much discussion and thoughtful analysis. In nearly any group, expect that there will be a range of opinions about grades, grading procedures, and the very meaning of assessment. I suggest that the group members do some reading about assessment before beginning the dialogue. Creating common ground for this topic will reduce time spent in useless debates where everyone ends up defending a point of view. In the interest of time, the articles could be jigsawed. Ask members to read articles from *Educational Leadership*'s Effective Grading Practices special issue (November 2011) and essays from leaders in the field in the book *Ahead of the Curve: The Power of Assessment to Transform Teaching and Learning* (Reeves, 2007).

2. Create and share a list of questions to guide members as they read, perhaps discussing one at each meeting.

   a. What is the purpose of assessment?
   b. What is the purpose of grades? How do we use grades in our school, grade level, or department?
   c. How do we assess for learning? What practices are effective? Ineffective?
   d. What assessments do we use? What are the advantages and disadvantages of each?
   e. How can we create meaningful assessments in our content area, grade group, or team?

In the meeting

3. After members read, discuss, and reach a consensus about how they can use assessment for increasing learning, the real work begins. With a partner or with the whole group, develop assessments for a particular topic of study. You may want to begin with textbook assessments that you have found to be effective and look at them in light of your new understanding about assessment.

In the classroom

4. Give the assessment to students and take the completed assessment to the next group meeting.

In the follow-up meeting

5. Discuss how the results of the assessment can be used to inform your instruction. In other words, what will your instruction look like based on the assessment? How will assignments be developed? Your group may wish to tweak the assessment for another teacher to use. Consider, also, how you will manage redos of this assessment. See Appendix B, Lesson Study Essentials, to help you with this process.

Once your group enters into this authentic assessment process, you can expect increased learning from students, more targeted instruction for teachers, and, as an added bonus, higher test scores.

7

Give It Up for Text Sets

When I consider all the issues related to textbook fatigue, none is more detrimental to the health of learning than the pressure teachers feel to cover, cover, cover—as if coverage rather than learning were the goal. Teachers know their content and want students to become passionate about the concepts that build and infuse their disciplines. Teachers become discouraged, however, when they look at the vast amount of content taunting them from the many pages of their teacher editions—and come close to having a panic attack when they count the days left in the year and the topics left to "cover."

I argue that it is the reliance on textbooks as a single source of curriculum, as well as standards that are far too broad and prescriptive, that creates this situation. Once districts invest in textbooks, along with their guaranteed alignment to state or Common Core State Standards, it is simply convenient to follow the yellow brick road beginning with Chapter 1. This "perceived expectation to teach to all of the standards and march through designated textbooks leads to superficial 'coverage' of instruction content. Numerous studies have documented that coverage is the rule rather than the exception in American education. Many of these studies have noted the ill effects of coverage" (McTighe & Seif, 2010, p. 154).

I worry that we are trying to stuff so much information into our students' heads that they have no time to digest it. The National Research Council confirmed this fear when they reported, "Curricula that emphasize an excessively broad range of subjects run the risk of developing disconnected rather than connected knowledge" (2000, p. 153). They state clearly, "More than ever, the sheer magnitude of human knowledge renders its coverage by education an impossibility" (2000, p. 5).

Many high-achieving countries have replaced the wide coverage of material with more focused, in-depth study. Even in mathematics, researchers are now finding that in countries such as Japan, students spend an hour working on one or two conceptual problems rather than trying to cover many topics as we do in the United States (Schoenfeld, 2008). McTighe and Seif report that 8th grade math teachers in the United States spend more time having their students solve problems than understanding the underlying mathematical principles. It is not that U.S. teachers don't want to engage students in deep, thoughtful learning. "The current curriculum simply contains too many topics and is too fragmented, often without clear connections from one topic or one level to the next" (McTighe & Seif, 2010, p. 155).

Deep study instead of broad coverage can be accomplished more easily when teachers do two things:

1. Focus collaboratively on how to help students apply knowledge within and across disciplines.
2. Use the textbook as one of many resources to help students learn concepts rather than only facts.

I realize that it's easy to say that students need access to a range of reading materials to build conceptual understandings, but how is a teacher to choose from the millions of resources available, especially online? One way is by working with colleagues to build text sets.

What Is a Text Set?

A text set is a collection of materials, usually created by the teacher (or media specialist), composed of diverse resources on a specific subject matter, genre, or theme. Text sets can include information from online sources or can be print-based, and a good text set offers materials at various reading levels. Once you begin to build a text set, perhaps in conjunction with a topic in the textbook, it takes on a life of its own that is similar to the experience of hearing a word for the first time and then hearing and seeing it *everywhere.* As you begin to gather books and articles for your collection, you will find resources on your topic at every turn. Soon you will have a rich spectrum of materials to supplement the textbook. Items to consider including in your text set:

- Articles from print periodicals or digital sources
- Books, often a range of fiction and nonfiction (print and digital)
- Radio broadcasts
- Poetry
- Short stories
- Primary documents, such as letters or diaries
- Lab results
- Data
- Songs (music or lyrics)
- Interviews
- Political cartoons
- Photographs or illustrations
- Government documents
- Blogs or tweets
- Student writing
- Picture books

- Maps, graphs, charts
- Lists of pertinent or related items
- Videos
- Biographies
- Art
- Plays
- Books with short texts, including almanacs

Multitext schools are familiar with text sets because they rely on them for their lessons. Many language arts teachers abandon whole class novels and collect text sets on themes such as heroes, coming of age, or internal conflict; they also collect genres such as mysteries or memoirs. Social studies teachers have an advantage because so many historical documents, photographs, music, and other artifacts are available online. As such, it is fairly easy to put together a set on slavery, the Industrial Revolution, or the U.S. presidency. And, increasingly, math and science teachers are finding a large selection of texts from which to choose on topics ranging from angles to cells.

In upper grades, students often contribute to text sets as they find materials in their own reading or researching. When I created a text set on epidemics, for example, students brought me fiction and nonfiction articles as well as recommendations of movies, songs, and photographs that fit the theme. Watch out, though. Students often get so enthusiastic that they bring you some things (especially in science) that you may not *want* in your text set.

How to Create a Text Set

Despite it sounding like a free-for-all, the creation of a text set is really quite deliberate. Many English and social studies teachers begin their text sets by thinking through various perspectives on a subject, such as war or family. The Annenberg Foundation offers a workshop on using text sets (http://www.learner.org/workshops/tml/workshop4/teaching.html) and in it teacher educator Jerome Harste suggests asking questions on a topic before seeking materials. "What would a psychologist want us to know about immigration? A geographer? A sociologist? An anthropologist? . . . How might the perspectives of a mother, a sister, and a daughter differ?" Harste advises that teachers ask "Whose story isn't being represented in the materials I've found? How can I add this voice/perspective?" (Danticat, Na, Yep, & others, 2012). These various points of view can't be shown in a single text, and students need the experience of various accounts to understand how they differ.

In addition, you may want to guide students toward specific learning goals by deliberately placing items in the text set that will support your points of instruction. A 4th grade writing teacher created a text set of books, articles, and online pieces that demonstrated to students how to begin their own writing in an interesting way. A middle school social studies teacher provided fiction books about the gold rush to help students build background knowledge, and later brought in a text set of nonfiction books and primary documents to correct misperceptions.

Benefits of Text Sets

One reason that many teachers favor text sets is that they make the content accessible to all students, especially those who struggle with reading. I have also found that readers may begin with a lower-level text, such as Will Hobbs's novel on immigration, *Crossing the Wire* (2006), or the picture book *Who Belongs Here? An American Story* (Knight, 2003) and move rather quickly to more challenging texts, often nonfiction, such as the cover piece in *Time,* "A New Line in the Sand" (Von Drehle, 2008), about the billion-dollar barrier that is going up between the United States and Mexico to control the flow of illegal immigrants. I also include poetry from and about immigrants and encourage immigrant students to add to my collection. Students may not have been motivated to approach a difficult piece of text such as the one in *Time* or try out poetry if they had not first read Hobbs's novel and gained prior knowledge as well as interest in the subject.

Especially now, as the Common Core State Standards (CCSS) are demanding more from readers, it is important to offer a wide variety of texts that allow students to practice skills such as synthesizing and critical reading. As Calkins, Ehrenworth, and Lehman point out, "Classrooms that have depended on excerpts, anthologies, and textbooks will find themselves needing to extend their libraries with literature and, for older students, primary and secondary sources." They go on to say that if students are using only textbooks, "they can't really analyze the warrant and reasoning that back up authors' claims, or compare craft, structure, and perspective; everything is already a summary" (2012, p. 30).

Perhaps one of the most beneficial aspects of text sets is that they engage students in reading. Think of a text set as similar to a book series, such as Harry Potter, Twilight, or The Hunger Games. When kids get hooked on a topic (or a book series), they keep reading. Our job is to provide enough text in different genres and at various reading levels so that they find themselves engaged before they remember to say that reading is boring. When students read, they boost comprehension and vocabulary skills, increase background knowledge, gain a broader view of the world, come to see themselves as intellectual beings, develop empathy, and guess what? They also score better on standardized tests.

Working Together with Text Sets

I was recently in the classroom of an 8th grade reading teacher who was using a popular reading intervention program. The district had spent a great deal of money for students to have access to this program, and many students had made gains. Despite that fact, the teacher felt that some students, especially those who had been using the program for more than a year, needed additional supplemental reading materials based on their interests and abilities. She was counseled by the reading coach, however, to adhere strictly to the program to achieve optimal results. The teacher had earned a master's degree in reading and had been teaching reading for many years, but she was convinced that her knowledge should be subjugated to a program that must know better about her students and their educational needs. Unfortunately, this scenario is repeated far too often.

Imagine for a moment a utopian educational world. The reading teacher is part of an interdisciplinary team that integrates instruction and talks each day about curriculum and resources. Furthermore, she knows all the topics of study in the students' other classes. This reading teacher brings her concern to the team, and the members help her create a text set of materials to support the topics of study, say a crossover picture book, *George vs. George: The American Revolution as Seen From Both Sides* (Schanzer, 2007), or, for more advanced readers, *The Secret of Sarah Revere* (Rinaldi, 1995), a young adult novel written from the perspective of Paul Revere's daughter. The teacher may include some primary documents from the social studies textbook. The science teacher might suggest a biography of a scientist, perhaps Benjamin Franklin since he lived during the time of the American Revolution, or a nonfiction book on electricity. The reading teacher, with her knowledge of the students' abilities and challenges, would then use the texts to teach reading skills and to support content-area study.

Some publishing companies capitalize on the idea of text sets by creating thematic sets of books, both fiction and nonfiction. With time and support, however, teams can work together to develop their own text sets that specifically meet the needs of their particular population of students. Figure 7.1 shows how a team of interdisciplinary teachers might develop a text set on the topic of the Dust Bowl.

Resources for Creating Text Sets

When looking for print texts, begin with your own professional education organizations and then broaden your search. Check with your media specialist about books that may be featured by your state's chapter of the American Library Association. The

7.1 Sample Text Set on Dust Bowl

Young adult fiction

- *Out of the Dust* (Hesse, 1997, 240 pages). Written in first-person free-verse poems, this Newbery Award winner is told from the point of view of a young girl who lives in the Dust Bowl during the Great Depression. Although the reading level is low, the concepts are mature.
- *The Green Coat: A Tale of the Dust Bowl Years* (McDunn, 2007, 200 pages). A 12-year-old girl is faced with tragedy when dust storms roll across North Dakota. An inspirational story of family, courage, and perseverance. Easy to read.

Biography

- *Farming the Dust Bowl: A First-hand Account from Kansas* (Svobida, 1986, 256 pages). Biographical account of a farmer who lived through the Dust Bowl is gripping and factual, but it will take older or more advanced younger readers to stay with it. The concepts are good for science teachers who want students to examine the ecological causes of the Dust Bowl.

Nonfiction, young adult

- *Children of the Dustbowl: The True Story of the School at Weedpatch Camp* (Stanley, 1993, 96 pages). A true story about the children of Dust Bowl migrant laborers who were sent to a farm-labor camp. It is an easy read and has illustrations. The camp was featured in Steinbeck's *Grapes of Wrath*, so American literature teachers may find the book a nice addition to their classroom libraries.

Photo essay

- *The Dust Bowl Through the Lens: How Photography Revealed and Helped Remedy a National Disaster* (Sandler, 2009, 96 pages). A wonderful example of visual literacy, this brings together famous and not-so-famous photographs of this disaster. It offers two-page spreads with a quote to begin each new topic along with a few paragraphs of text. Use this book for language arts, science, and social studies; it explores how farming methods and the weather contributed to the Great Depression.

Nonfiction

- *The Worst Hard Time: The Untold Story of Those Who Survived the Great American Dust Bowl* (Egan, 2006, 340 pages). As the most difficult read in the text set, this book is also the most graphic and comprehensive for students who develop a keen interest in the topic or need a bit of a challenge.

Websites

- **Surviving the Dustbowl (PBS documentary and website).** The website previews the video and offers interviews, biographies, and articles related to the Dust Bowl. A section on the website asks viewers to share their experience, especially if they knew someone who lived during this time. Retrieved from http://www.pbs.org/wgbh/americanexperience/films/dustbowl/
- **Library of Congress American Memory.** Search this website for "dust bowl" and you'll find 118 items, mostly photographs, but it also includes manuscripts from the Federal Writers' Project. Take a look at http://memory.loc.gov/ammem/index.html.
- **Wessels Living History Museum of York, Nebraska.** Students can choose a real person who survived the Dust Bowl and listen to his story at www.livinghistoryfarm.org/farminginthe30s/water_02.html
- **National Weather Service: The Black Sunday Dust Storm of 14 April 1935.** Site offers weather data for April 14, 1935 (Black Sunday) along with reports of the great dust storm. For information, visit http://www.srh.noaa.gov/oun/?n=blacksunday
- **Woody Guthrie.** Hear Woody Guthrie sing "Dusty Old Dust," a song he made famous about a dust storm at http://www.youtube.com/watch?v=t4MOHF19tJw. The lyrics may be retrieved from http://woodyguthrie.org/Lyrics/So_Long_Its_Been_Good.htm

ALA chapters often create lists of outstanding books for children and young adults. For example, ALA Florida offers a list of best young adult novels each year, voted on by teen readers. The Sunshine State Young Readers Awards for grades 3–5 and 6–8 are also voted on by students. Here are those and other great websites to help you find books that will appeal to your students and complement your content area.

- Florida American Library Association's awards for teen readers—www.floridamedia.org/?page=Flo_Teen_Past_Win
- Sunshine State Young Readers Awards for grades 3–5, and 6–8—http://myssyra.org
- Young Adult Library Services—www.ala.org/yalsa/booklist
- Coretta Scott King Book Awards—www.ala.org/emiert/cskbookawards
- Notable Children's Books—www.ala.org/alsc/awardsgrants/notalists
- Outstanding Books for the College Bound—www.ala.org/yalsa/booklists/obcb
- Best Books for Young Adults—www.ala.org/yalsa/booklists/bbya
- Orbis Pictus Awards for Outstanding Nonfiction for Children—www.ncte.org/awards/orbispictus
- National Book Award Winners—www.nationalbook.org/
- Hispanic Heritage Month Recommended Reading List—www.justreadfamilies.org/Reading/HHM.asp

Online Resources

As you look to online sources for additions to your text sets, stick to websites that are consistently reliable and comprehensive. Content-area teachers have found the following websites to be helpful.

- Federal Resources for Educational Excellence (FREE) at http://free.ed.gov. This website is a collection of materials sponsored by the U.S. Department of Education. It offers free teacher resources from various federal agencies, divided into content and specialty areas including music and life sciences.

- Library of Congress at www.loc.gov has thousands of primary documents, and the teacher page at www.loc.gov/teachers highlights ready-to-use classroom materials. The American Memory page at http://memory.loc.gov/ammem/index.html is invaluable for social studies teachers.
- NASA's web page at http://www.nasa.gov includes a section for teachers that offers everything you always wanted to know about NASA's various missions.
- PBS Teachers at http://www.pbs.org/teachers is a go-to website for all content areas. You'll find TV programming, multimedia web content, and lesson plans.
- The National Science Digital Library at http://www.nsdl.org is the nation's online library for education and research in science, technology, engineering, and mathematics. Look for STEM-related resources here.
- Teachers' Domain at http://www.teachersdomain.org offers free digital media from public TV broadcasters for educational use.
- WatchKnowLearn at http://watchknowlearn.org/default.aspx offers free educational videos from 2,000 categories.

Text Set Tips

Incorporate student-created contributions from present and previous students such as writing, illustrations, poetry, and music. Students enjoy seeing the work of peers, so these items are usually highly engaging.

Have students preview the chapter in a textbook and come up with items they would like to find in a text set. This assignment is a great way to provide purpose for the topic as well as to engage students in the text.

Allow students to print photographs, song lyrics, and other items to place on a bulletin board to develop their ownership and pride in the topic while immersing them in the learning.

Include reading materials across broad levels and don't worry about placing items in the set that may seem too easy or too difficult. As students gain interest, they will move to appropriate ability levels.

Put out a call to parents and other teachers to let them know when you are creating a text set. You'll be surprised what is out there that you may have overlooked once you invite others to participate.

Community of Practice: Creating Text Sets

Any group that collaborates on text sets has a relatively easy task that will reap great rewards in student comprehension and engagement. For this learning community activity, you may work within your own discipline or across disciplines, depending upon your purpose for developing a text set. Following is a suggested outline for the group's activities, although most of the activities could be done alone or informally as well.

Before the meeting

1. Look through the curriculum or textbook and find topics that lend themselves to text sets. Eventually, you will want text sets for every topic, but start slow so you don't become overwhelmed.
2. Consider giving your media specialist advance notice of the meeting. Invite her to attend and offer some background information on text sets as well as lists of books, periodicals, and websites in various disciplines.

In the meeting

3. Once your group decides on a topic for a text set, brainstorm items that would be appropriate for a text set. Textbooks sometimes offer suggestions of texts (especially young adult fiction and nonfiction) that relate to the topic.
4. Consider listing categories of items, such as primary documents or articles, to help you remember to include an array of genres in your text set.

5. Decide if you want students, other teachers, parents, or the community at large to contribute to this text set and, if so, what criteria you will establish for inclusion of items, as well as how you will manage the contributions. For example, some items may be only on loan and others will be donated to the set. Consider placing a team of students in charge of the text set.
6. Discuss how you can best use the text sets, such as for independent or required reading, research, or to support planned activities.
7. Design a collaborative activity using the text set, perhaps having students work in pairs to share a summary of a book, present a primary document, answer essential questions using targeted websites, or discuss the significance of an artifact.

In the classroom

8. Talk to students about how text sets are used to deepen the study of any topic by providing more information than would be found in a typical textbook. Show students each resource in the text set and explain why it is important to the unit of study. Engage students in the following activity to help them become familiar with text sets.

    a. Place students in small groups and ask each group what else they would like to see in the text set.
    b. Ask them to explain how the additional item would further learning about the topic.
    c. Have them share their ideas with the class.

9. Use the collaborative activity that you created in your meeting (#7). Afterward, ask students how their learning increased by using multiple resources instead of only the textbook.

In the follow-up meeting

10. Discuss students' responses to the text set and make notes of any good ideas that students may have had for adding to the text set. Share observations regarding the collaborative activity and talk about how it could be improved for the next lesson.

Resources for Creating Text Sets

Artifactual Literacies: Every Object Tells a Story by K. Pahl and J. Rowsell

Reading Ladders: Leading Students from Where They Are to Where We'd Like Them to Be by T. Lesesne

The Reading Zone: How to Help Kids Become Skilled, Passionate, Habitual, Critical Readers by N. Atwell

When Textbooks Fall Short: New Ways, New Texts, New Sources of Information in the Content Areas by N. Walker, T. W. Bean, and B. Dillard

8

Going From Textbook Fatigue to Invigorated Learning

Pull into the parking lot of Da Vinci Academy, a branch of South Hall Middle School in Gainesville, Georgia, and you'll see a nondescript building that looks like it has seen lots of kids over the years. There is nothing special about the building; nothing foretells what you'll find inside. As you enter the double glass doors, however, you become immediately aware that this is a place where things *happen:* a brightly colored, hand-painted scene of jungle animals surrounds the doorway of the first classroom, a sign points the way to the Museum Store, and through a glass door you can see a real café that looks like it was imported from Paris. And that's just at first glance.

On my tour, I walked through an organic garden maintained by the science classes, a boys' bathroom with Greek mythology characters painted bigger than life on each wall (as well as over the urinals), and, no kidding, a real museum featuring an Out of Africa exhibit that the 7th graders in all content areas have been working on for several weeks. The exhibits include galleries where visitors can explore the diseases of Africa and the available immunizations. A student dressed as a nurse explains what vaccines are available and how they work. Another section has been transformed into a marketplace where herbs and other goods are displayed for potential consumers, and around the corner you can use a Wii to experience the music and dances of Africa. What looks to be a real sarcophagus, on loan from a local antique store, is in an area that promises to be popular, especially if visitors stop to listen as a student describes in great detail the process of mummification. Each display is staffed by students who have become experts in their field, and they are preparing for visitors, elementary children and community members, who will tour the museum on a specified day. Student-produced brochures are featured at each exhibit, and a viewer's guide on the wall reflects research that students have conducted on their topic. And since this is a modern museum, visitors can scan QR codes with their cell phones. I learned a lot on my tour, especially at the geography station where I discovered, I am embarrassed to admit, that the Serengeti is merely a region of Africa—not a specific country. I asked many questions of this student expert since African geography obviously isn't my forte; he answered them all as if he had been studying this subject for years instead of only weeks.

Soon Out of Africa will be dismantled and the 6th grade students will prepare their exhibit, Against All Odds. Their theme incorporates natural disasters (weather) as well as manmade disasters (environmental issues) in settings including Australia and Canada. All 6th grade teachers will work together to make sure that concepts from every discipline are woven into the research and production.

Cindy White, teacher at Da Vinci Academy, coordinates the exhibits in the museum and teaches an elective for students who are interested in the project. As a science teacher, Ms. White always had science artifacts in her classroom and simply expanded the concept to include the entire school. She calls the museum the "ultimate learning center" and says that such museums can be created by any school that wants to "go for it."

It Looks Like . . .

I've always believed that engagement can be sensed when one first enters a school or classroom; it is an almost tangible element that leaps out at you and captures your own interest, and this experience confirmed my belief. As I wandered from classroom to classroom, I saw and *felt* the engagement of both students and teachers. In a social studies class, for example, Melissa Madsen's students were creating maps of Africa using various colored salt dough to designate different countries. Printed maps were glued inside boxes donated by a local pizza company so they could be safely stacked. Students did not notice when I entered; they continued working in small groups, using the instructions provided by the teacher to complete the project. Ms. Madsen explained that students will choose a country in Africa and gain core knowledge through a web quest. Afterward, students will present their findings using various media, including classroom wall murals, electronic murals, multimedia public service announcements, and an i-movie. They will also participate in a Socratic circle, where they will discuss a big question, such as, "What are some solutions to Africa's deforestation?"

I asked Ms. Madsen how much time it took to come up with such units. "These projects do initially take time, but once created, it is just a matter of refining the lesson for future students." She works with other teachers to make the lessons as integrated as possible. Her students worked on several units this year, one focused on the Middle East. In this unit, students chose a country, researched its water issues, and participated in a water summit as an activist for their country. During the summit, representatives outlined the major water issues in their country, debated who should have access to the limited water supply, posed questions to other countries, and offered solutions. The teacher acted as a facilitator, stepping back to allow the students an opportunity to interact in the role-play situation, complete with costumes and accents. She remembers that Israel and Jordan had a particularly engaging exchange.

Ms. Madsen's units adhere to the district curriculum frameworks and state standards, and like all teachers, she feels she gets behind at times. "I realize that not all lessons can involve a project or simulation; there is just not enough time to have an activity for each concept or standard. Sometimes a lesson can be given using a brief PowerPoint presentation and short lecture, but because my students learn so much better through hands-on teaching, I develop my units to include project-based lessons and activities that connect to real world issues."

As I went from class to class, I could see that this was a guiding principle of the school as a whole. In science, students were watching their teacher, Sara Atwill, model the digestive process with a slippery and unappealing hot dog, a blender, a short pipe, a jug, and a long flexible tube that represented the small intestine. In groups, the students filled out charts using the correct anatomical vocabulary as they exclaimed aloud that the whole process was "totally gross." I suspect they will forever remember where their food goes when they chew it and exactly how it gets there.

What interested me the most was the intrinsic motivation evidenced by the questions the students asked. "Now what does the pancreas do again?" one student asked the teacher, but before she could answer, another student in the group reminded him of its role. Ms. Atwill commented that she has few print textbooks but that she likes using web searches with online textbooks. "They provide good science links. The publishers have narrowed down the websites about the human body, for example, to about ten instead of a million."

I observed the same type of learning in math where students were using computers to answer an essential question that had been posted on the board: "How can I measure surface area and volume of irregular shapes?" The teacher, Ley Hathcock, moved around the room answering questions and encouraging the young mathematicians to go deeper. One student asked, "How many problems do I have to do?"

Mr. Hathcock replied, "How many have you done?"

"Three."

"Why don't you do a couple more and make sure they are harder than the ones you've already completed."

"OK," the student answered and turned back to his computer. Since math is often a subject in which teachers rely heavily on the textbook, I asked Mr. Hathcock about his class's textbook use. He said that he follows the standards but was able to compress them and use them only as guides for teaching.

"My goal is to have students go through a process instead of memorizing a formula. I want them to use information to solve real-world problems." He said the students may use textbooks to look up something or to get ideas but they do not go through them step by step.

Every teacher I talked to said the same thing regarding textbook use. Textbooks were simply one resource in a vast repertoire of sources from which they could create lessons. One classroom had several copies of teacher editions but no student editions; another class had a few student editions in the resource section of the class library; the science classes used online textbooks at times, and the language arts teachers sometimes had students read short stories from the textbook.

It is not just the lack of textbooks that creates such a learning environment, of course, but a common understanding that students need to synthesize and adapt all sorts of information to further understandings as they solve problems and manipulate learning in authentic settings. As Linda Darling-Hammond reminds us, "Twenty-first century students need a deeper understanding of the core concepts in the disciplines than they receive now. In addition, students need to be able to design, evaluate, and manage their own work. Students need to be able to frame, investigate, and solve problems using a wide range of information resources and digital tools" (2010b, p. 33–34). In my quest to analyze schools that are moving toward that ideal, I have discovered several commonalities.

From Transmission to Exploration

In the transmission model, teachers and textbooks are seen as the receptacle of knowledge; as such they decide what students need to know and then transmit that information directly to them, much like downloading a file to your computer. Although we have more engaging media than we have had in the past, lecture is still lecture, even if it is accompanied by a PowerPoint presentation; passive learning is still passive learning. Unfortunately, the purpose of this sort of transmission is often to enable students to pass a test, allow teachers to cover the standards, or get everyone through the textbook's table of contents.

Inquiry-Based Learning

The inquiry, or problem-based model, a hallmark of schools that use multiple texts, turns the transmission approach on its head. It creates a reason for learning material, a purpose for study by tapping into that universal phenomenon called curiosity. Students work from the stance of wanting to know and becoming deeply engaged in learning because it has an authentic outcome.

At Da Vinci Academy, the English teachers create online book clubs where students across classes can blog about the books they are reading. Teachers sponsor two literary lunches per book where students come together physically to discuss a question posed by the teachers. In the 7th grade class, for example, the question associated with reading books about dystopias asks, "What can go wrong in a dystopia?"

Kristy Cossett at Rashkis Elementary School in Chapel Hill, North Carolina, describes how 4th grade students create their own cereal boxes in an integrated unit by developing the nutritional formulas that they would want in their cereals. She says, "Instead of having them open up the textbooks and go through each lesson, we do activities that support the information in the textbooks. In this case, students must figure out proportions and use decimals to create the nutritional information for the cereal." The intrinsic motivation in these activities keeps kids reading, talking, and thinking.

Indeed, this type of instruction, a component of 21st century learning, seems to be catching on nationally. John Barell, author of several books about inquiry and problem-based learning, explains the approach in this way:

> It encompasses a rethinking of the entire curriculum so that teachers design whole units around complex 'ill-structured' problematic scenarios that embody the major concepts to be mastered and understood. By 'ill-structured' or 'ill-defined' I mean the realistic, authentic problems—such as pollution of the planet and feeding the hungry—that are so complex, messy, and intriguing that they do not lend themselves to a right or wrong answer approach. (2010, p. 178)

Although there are many models for engaging in inquiry, Harvey and Daniels created a succinct and eminently doable model of the process:

- Immerse: Invite curiosity, build background, find topics, and wonder
- Investigate: Develop questions, search for information, and discover answers
- Coalesce: Intensify research, synthesize information, and build knowledge
- Go public: Share learning, demonstrate understanding, take action. (2009, pp. 61–62)

Clearly, engaging in inquiry is not possible when moving from one chapter to the next in a textbook; however, *using* information in a textbook, along with other sources, can certainly form the foundation for inquiry projects.

Proponents of such active learning make a clear distinction between inquiry-based learning and student-centered projects. Jeff Wilhelm makes this distinction. "To qualify as inquiry, a project must build upon and apply disciplinary understanding"

(2007, p. 13). When I mentioned to Paula Stubbs, principal of Da Vinci Academy, that the students responded well to this hands-on approach, she told me that they preferred to think of this type of learning as "minds on." "I didn't make up that term," she said, "but that's what we aspire to. We want students thinking, not just doing."

When students created their traveling museum boxes in Teresa Haymore's language arts class, they didn't simply look around for objects related to the topic and stick them in a box or create a diorama that often amounts to little more than an art project. I talked to the two girls who had created a box on the Taj Mahal as a result of reading about it, and they explained to me how they became interested in the topic, what they wanted to know as they researched it, and how their project would help other students understand the concept behind the Taj Mahal as well as the country of India. Inside the box they placed an original short story about the building of the Taj Mahal, an original poem about India, and an illustrated book they coauthored using Mixbook (www.mixbook.com/edu). They also included fiction and nonfiction books, models of the building, and pictures representing the culture of India both inside and outside the large wooden box. The box wasn't just for a grade, either, as the intended audience is students at other schools studying India.

Project-Based Learning

Project-based learning (PBL), similar to inquiry-based learning, is becoming popular in traditional as well as "textbook-free" schools. With PBL, students begin with the vision of a product (or presentation) that creates a context and reason for researching and learning new information.

In Ben Davis High School in Indianapolis, for example, all teachers are engaged in PBL and are expected to facilitate at least one project per semester in their discipline. They work from content standards and make sure the projects require critical thinking, problem solving, collaboration, and communication. A driving question is at the heart of the model, and students must come up with something new, such as an idea, offer a different interpretation, or create a product. Projects are much like the senior project required for graduation in many schools in that both are often presented to a panel or an authentic audience, made up of community members or professionals in the field. The district's PBL director, Steven Loser, says that teachers at Ben Davis are at various stages in the implementation of this model. In a school with more than 3,000 students, that is no surprise. As expected, textbooks are used as only one of many resources in the project.

Project-based learning is common in Singapore, as well, where students "study plants, animals, and insects in the school's eco-garden; they run their own recycling center, they write and edit scripts for the Internet radio program they produce; and they use handheld computers to play games and create mathematical models that develop their quantitative abilities" (Darling-Hammond, 2010a, p. 6). PBL is also the touchstone of learning in one of the highest performing nations, Finland. Dan Rather takes a close look at the Finnish school system in which students learn actively by doing projects such as dissecting a heart and testing their own blood types in a high school science class in place of memorizing information (Rather, 2012).

Why the move toward this type of learning? One reason could be that a number of studies have found that students engaged in a problem-oriented curriculum exhibited increased learning on standardized tests and performance assessments (Barron & Darling-Hammond, 2008, p. 64). And then there is the intense engagement and deep learning that is evident in schools that embrace this approach.

Student Collaboration

Although some textbook activities encourage collaboration, the vast majority of questions and activities fall into the transmission approach to instruction. Collaboration is seen as an activity unto itself; a deviation in the school as usual day. Students are directed to participate in a collaborative activity, usually for a grade given by their teacher, and then they return to the read and answer questions model. In contrast, successful collaboration is evidenced by the following:

- Students are involved in discussions as contributors and responders.
- The contributions are coordinated instead of consisting of many independent conversations.
- Students are generally on-task.
- Students' eye gaze and body movement indicate attention (Barron & Darling-Hammond, 2008).

In schools that use textbooks as resources, student collaboration underlies most learning. In nearly every such school that I've visited, I observed students arranged in pods or seated at tables. They work together, do projects together, use technology together, and learn together.

Schools of the future are being designed and built to facilitate such communal learning. In Megan Lewis's 6th grade English class at Da Vinci Academy, desks and tables were replaced with sofas and comfortable canvas folding chairs. Instead of one large area, Ms. Lewis's classroom is made up of three smaller rooms. Students gather in their groups in different rooms to read, rearrange themselves in book club communities for a quick discussion, and then meet together in the blue room for minilessons and whole-group sharing. The lesson that I observed was interesting in many ways, but I was most fascinated with the dexterity with which the students moved into and out of different groups and immediately got to work. In one case, they had only five minutes to discuss the similarities of characters in a short story before reassembling for whole-group sharing. During the share-out session, it was clear that they had gained understanding because the list of characteristics they put together was detailed and thought-provoking.

The National Research Council discusses the substantial benefits of such community-centered classrooms in the book *How*

People Learn: Brain, Mind, Experience, and School. In the book, the authors point out that outside the classroom "much learning and problem solving takes place as individuals engage with each other, inquire of those with skills and expertise, and use resources and tools that are available in the surrounding environment" (2000, p. 279). This "distributed cognition" can be transferred to the classroom, as evidenced by Ms. Lewis's approach to teaching. In a study representing more than eight decades of research with 17,000 early adolescents from 11 countries, results indicate that there is higher achievement and more positive peer relationships when students engage in cooperative rather than competitive or individual structures (Roseth, Johnson, & Johnson, 2008).

Respect and Relationships

One of the most significant aspects of schools of inquiry is that students learn the art of collaboration rather than the often artificial group work. They come to value the contributions of their peers and rely on each other to fill in the gaps. When I was sponsor of the school newspaper, I saw firsthand how relationships and respect grow from embedded collaboration. Students had a purpose for their investigation, and they worked with each other to accomplish their goals of interviewing, writing, taking photographs, and researching. Although they might not always agree (in fact, I witnessed some powerful intellectual arguments), they learned how to work with one another in a way that was respectful because they truly did honor each other's contributions. They understood the value of their peers in making the final product exceptional and trusted each other to do their part. I was not surprised when a former student contacted me and said that the relationships created on that newspaper staff continue today.

In the 6th grade English class I mentioned earlier, students put their names on a list if they needed a conference with their teacher. Ms. Lewis would call them from their groups, one at a time, and talk quietly with them at her conference table. I asked the teacher if I could sit in on a conference and she immediately turned to the student and inquired if that would be OK with her. I was chagrined that I hadn't asked the student first myself, but old habits die hard. I found this intrinsic respect of others' efforts a defining quality of the school. The work belonged to the students, not to the teachers, and this acknowledgement fostered a sense of pride in its production.

Fostering Trust

In schools following the inquiry approach, I didn't see charts on classroom walls that told students what they could or could not do, such as "No gum chewing," "No hats," or the ubiquitous "Come to class prepared." Certainly, there were no signs demanding "No talking." When there were rules posted, they were created by students and differed according to each classroom. I also saw bottles of water on student desks, an indication that those in charge acknowledge that kids get thirsty and, like all of us, might learn better if they can take a sip of water as they learn. The sense of democracy and of respect was palpable.

In all the schools I visited that use textbooks as a resource, I was amazed at the neat condition of the schools, even though some of the buildings were older and had not been updated in years. In one huge high school, located in a low-socioeconomic community in Southern Florida, I noticed that there was no litter on the grounds and no graffiti in the students' bathrooms. When I asked the principal why students were so respectful of the school, he said simply, "Kids don't damage what belongs to them." Indeed, there was evidence that the staff trusted students to make it theirs: lunch tables outside, students moving among classrooms without passes as they worked on interdisciplinary projects, service learning projects where students made decisions about the process, and murals painted by students on walls and even ceilings. In sad contrast, I visited a large, inner-city high school where the message was "We don't trust you to do anything right, and we're not taking any chances on you either." Police officers were stationed at the entry doors, metal detectors scanned students upon entering, strict rules made by staff were imposed on students, and a lock-down environment permeated the entire building. These students didn't have the opportunity to earn trust, much less be given it.

In the news piece produced by Dan Rather on Finnish schools, one of the administrators he interviewed made the point that a key concept of their success is trust: officials trust principals, principals trust staff, staff trusts students, students trust each other. Interestingly, when I asked Ms. Stubbs, principal of Da Vinci Academy, what her advice would be for other administrators who wanted to take the leap into inquiry-based learning, her first response was, "Trust your teachers." Perhaps it is just a coincidence, but in my experience, it seems that when schools release their singular tie to textbooks, the unexpected element of trust seems to emerge and, like a self-fulfilling prophecy, wondrous things begin to happen.

Communities of Teachers

Another hallmark of teachers in schools with textbooks used only as resources is that they form strong communities because they rely on each other as they create lessons from various sources. In South Hall Middle School the assistant principal and science coach, Kent Townley, described how the 6th grade science teachers formed one of the best professional working groups he has ever seen. "As a result of this collaboration, they have now become a social community, doing things with their families on the weekends," he said. The social situation is a result of their common purpose in planning, organizing, and sharing responsibilities for 6th grade science lessons every day. "They meet kids where they are because they spend time tiering lessons and making sure they are flexible in meeting kids' needs." He called their work "frontloading," noting that during the first year the work is pretty intensive, but every year after, as teachers gather resources and create lessons, it becomes easier.

Teresa Haymore says that she spends a lot of time collaborating with another 7th grade language arts teacher in a different school. Together, they have developed ideas for projects, such as the traveling museum boxes, as well as concepts suitable for literature circles. In addition, they are finding ways to have their students work together. Collaboration, like seeds in a fertile field, keeps producing results.

Schools must make a firm commitment to providing time for teachers to plan together as they design lessons, share resources, and learn from one another. In schools where such time is not allocated, frustration and resentment replace innovation and synergy. In Ben Davis High School, where all teachers facilitate a project-based initiative in their classes, teachers are given an hour each week for planning purposes. In Rashkis Elementary, teachers are provided two hours once a month in addition to common planning for collaboration, and while they are grateful for this block of time, they acknowledge that it is not enough. South Hall Middle provides at least one hour each week for teachers to plan together. "They develop units, plan curriculum, and create assessments that follow the frameworks and state standards," said Paige Bagwell, the school's literacy coach.

In many high-achieving countries, schools allocate seven to fifteen days throughout the year for professional learning and provide five to ten hours a week "for teachers to plan and problem solve together around students and subject matter" (Darling-Hammond, 2010a, p. 261). These hours are in addition to their individual planning time.

As I noted in previous chapters, student collaboration leads to increased engagement as well as high performance, and many researchers have now identified teacher collaboration as the key element of successful schools, those defined as having high levels of student learning (Darling-Hammond, 2010a).

Teachers as Coaches

Inquiry-driven instruction attracts a certain type of teacher, a risk-taker who is comfortable with not always being in control of everything that may happen in a lesson. That kind of person knows how to be a facilitator, considers herself a learner, and doesn't let ego get in the way. Often such teachers are natural-born encouragers and coaches, pushing students to go deeper while validating their progress. These teachers ask questions rather than make demands, model rather than lecture, and participate rather than direct. I also found that they tend to use common language that asks rather than tells when working with students in small groups. Here are some examples of the language used by these teacher-coaches:

- What do you think?
- Can you explain . . . ?
- Why don't you try . . . ?
- Remember that . . . ?
- What would happen if . . . ?
- Why did you . . . ?
- What do you want to know about . . . ?
- What else should you include?
- Is there another way?
- Will you show (another student) how you did that?

Blue Ridge Elementary teacher Kate George has created a garden club in her school called "Cool Kids Grow." For this month's meeting, she brings in a guest speaker who is an environmentalist to talk about the water cycle. Ms. George's husband, a soil scientist, also came to discuss the soil that will go into the terrariums the members will be making. After the students listen to the speakers, she allows them to form groups and moves among them offering assistance with their terrariums, pointing out what might work, explaining the purpose of certain plants, asking them what they think. She is adept at bringing students into a circle of learning as she draws out their questions and guides them in understanding the *why* as well as the *what*. In her role as learning coach, she supports students as they use their new learning to transform themselves into scientists.

Jeff Wilhelm suggests that teachers who are moving away from the "information-transmission" model recast themselves as co-collaborators. He uses the metaphor of a road trip when describing their role. "Teachers and students take a collaborative journey toward disciplinary understanding. Exact destination unknown, but road maps and resources are valued, and specified navigation strategies are learned along the way. Teaching is authoritative (not authoritarian), participatory, collaborative. The teacher acts as a mentor and guide" (2007, p. 29).

Advantages of Textbook-free Schools

It would not be fair to say that schools using textbooks as resources have different expectations for their students. We all want students to learn deeply, think critically, apply new learning in various situations, solve problems, and develop civic responsibility. I can't help but believe, however, that students who have been educated in textbook-tied ways face disadvantages that are significant and long-lasting, especially in the 21st century where they are expected to work with others and approach problems creatively.

Students Become Critical Readers

Schools that provide a variety of resources teach students to be skeptical readers, writers, and listeners. Principal Paula Stubbs said their students are taught to question *everything* (her emphasis). Teresa Haymore said she had to laugh at a student who said in frustration "Nothing I learn here is true" after they had spent several days on a project where students had to question the accuracy of the material the teachers presented. Ms. Haymore describes a series of questions that she developed as a credibility meter to help her students determine if their sources were credible. Several students assured me when I was reading their work that they had put their sources through the meter. Because such schools use a variety of sources, they teach students to think about text in a new way. Teachers who use only the textbook don't feel the need to incorporate such skills because fact-checkers have done the work for students.

Textbook publishers are also often reluctant to take risks that are necessary in helping students learn from various perspectives.

Ms. Haymore described a project students did in her English class where they read about the Israeli-Palestinian conflict from three different perspectives. One book, *A Little Piece of Ground* (Laird, 2006), was told from the Palestinian perspective; another book, Ted Dekker's *Blink of an Eye* (2011), was from a Christian point of view; and the third, *A Bottle in the Gaza Sea* (Zenatti, 2008), was a balanced look at the conflict. Students discovered how texts on the same topic can vary widely depending upon the perspective of the author, and they were able to engage in meaningful discussions about how such perspectives may influence readers.

Students Become Independent Learners

Students who learn through inquiry, projects, and multiple texts become more independent simply because they must. They quickly understand that they have little choice but to take responsibility for their own learning and in schools where I've visited they do so with pleasure. In fact, some students become absolutely enthusiastic over their knowledge, eager to share with visitors what they've learned and obviously proud of their accomplishments. This is unlike some classes I've visited where students sit quietly at their desks with open textbooks. Often, students in such classes seem surprised when asked their opinions and look immediately at the text when asked a question.

Another characteristic of schools that approach learning through multiple sources is that students are encouraged to take a position on an issue, find evidence to support that position, and communicate their findings clearly. In an English class at Da Vinci Academy, for example, students had to decide if acronyms should be in the dictionary and argue their case. In Ms. Madsen's social studies class, students studied the Vietnam War and were then given cards that designated their role: reporter, draft dodger, hippie, scientist, hawk, or dove. They had to research their character and explain and defend the perspective that person would have of the war. Such miniprojects encourage independence and grow students' self-efficacy at the same time.

Students Learn through Interdisciplinary Instruction

Schools that use textbooks as resources have a tendency to have more interdisciplinary contact. Because teachers don't rely on single source textbooks, they move outside their disciplines to work in teams. At first the teachers at Ben Davis High School worked only within their disciplines on projects, but many teachers are now including other disciplines as they expand the breadth of projects. Knowledge doesn't come in neat little packages labeled "science," "social studies," "English," and "math," despite textbooks that seem to capture information in just that way. Ninth grade students reading *Animal Farm* (Orwell, 2003), for example, need to understand the Russian Revolution in order to gain any meaning from the novel, just as students reading *The Diary of a Young Girl* (Frank, 2010) need to have background knowledge about the Holocaust. What better way to provide that information than by integrating it through social studies and English classes?

I once met two teachers who taught math and English together, and they declared definitively that they would quit teaching if their partnership were discontinued. They told me that they loved working together, but more important to them, they felt that their students were learning so much more in the team-taught class than when they taught the subjects separately.

How to Make the Transition

Moving from a textbook-centered curriculum to one that uses a variety of resources takes planning and vision. Most schools or academies within schools begin by visiting sites that have successfully made the transition, finding elements that will work for them, and then reinventing the wheel. Every combination of staff, every group of students, every district, and every physical location is different, and the key is to find what works for you. Fortunately, unlike other initiatives, this one doesn't require a huge cash investment. Rather, it requires a new mindset and a group of people committed to change.

Find the Right Principal

It is absolutely essential for a school that is venturing toward inquiry-based learning to find the right principal. Principal Paula Stubbs always believed in the workshop approach, a sort of lab method of teaching with multiple sources where students collaborate and the teacher acts as a facilitator. Her core beliefs and experience allowed her to support teachers as they moved away from a textbook-regimented classroom. Today, you'll find her in teachers' classrooms, often as a participant in a lesson, and she asks lots of questions. "I thought it was interesting that you used that particular story," she said to an English teacher. "What made you chose it?" Her questions aren't criticisms; she just wants to know, and the teachers respond to her as they would a trusted ally.

That doesn't mean that she will let anyone off the hook if they aren't on board. "She has high expectations," Paige Bagwell said of her principal, "and teachers know it."

When I asked Ms. Stubbs how much cognitive dissonance there was when the staff first began the school, she said it took a lot of talking through issues. Teachers spent time imagining what such a school might look like and honestly discussing their fears. They learned to take "supported risks" and try on leadership roles.

Ms. Stubbs also discussed the importance of customized staff development based on students' needs and strengths in place of a generic model. Principals in such schools are active in staff development, and PLCs are not cookie-cutter affairs but rather customized learning communities that change according to the need. Student data, much of it informal and including student work samples and teacher observations, infuse professional meetings and principals allow teachers the autonomy to make decisions. Learning, not testing, is the focus of the principal and of the school as a whole.

Incorporate Community

Schools that have given up their reliance on the textbook tend to incorporate the community more than other schools because they are always looking for resources. Even in schools where parent involvement has been traditionally low, the school finds ways of making families a part of the culture. In Da Vinci Academy, community members and parents are accustomed to being asked to help, and they come through in unexpected ways, such as taking on the responsibility for the museum store.

Teachers are always looking for guest speakers and people with specialized experience, such as gardeners who are willing to help schools start a garden or experts in fields who will lend tools and advice. In a Florida school that created a law academy, local attorneys provided a law library and the local bar association members were available to tutor students.

With project-based learning, schools need authentic audiences, and community members are usually eager to share in the experience, acting as panelists to hear student presentations or as mentors to students who need additional assistance.

Not all schools are fortunate enough to have parents who are free to contribute a lot of time or a large community of professionals, but as schools move into the community, perhaps through service learning projects, the community will be more likely to return to them.

Collect Resources

Paige Bagwell said one of the hardest parts of moving away from textbooks as a single source is finding resources. The teachers are constantly on the prowl for resources that tie into their curriculum, and the Internet has become a valuable source, especially in recent years. Some teachers' workrooms may look like storage pods as they accumulate articles, books, and physical items, but it's worth the mess. Bagwell admits that often the best teachers in such schools are those with high organizational skills.

A good media center and unflappable media specialist is also a bonus in such schools, although Da Vinci Academy relies on the nearby city library. Bagwell said the media specialist in her middle school is constantly asked to put together text sets for topics or provide books related to a unit of study. When I was there, the library was a hive of activity with students using books and games in small groups and teachers stopping by to pick up materials.

In many of these types of schools, you won't find class sets of anything. The money available for resources (and in some cases, textbooks) is spent on purchasing five to ten copies of the same titles so students can read in small groups. Rashkis Elementary has a large reading room with article files, e-books, and magazines, as well as a wide variety of fiction and nonfiction books. Since the paradigm has shifted from whole class instruction to small group facilitation, there is no need for extensive copying of worksheets, handouts, or other class sets of materials. And Paula Stubbs says the money they save at Da Vinci on copying costs goes directly into buying the resources necessary to facilitate 'minds-on' learning.

Moving Toward the Future

I am convinced that learning such as I've described in this chapter will soon be the norm. We really don't have a choice if we hope to compete globally and give students the tools they will need to solve the difficult challenges that our society has laid at their doors. The days of learning everything there is to know about a subject went the way of the corded telephone and leaded gasoline. Information cannot be contained as it once was in a single volume or even in a single library: the Internet tore off the bindings and blew away the walls. Incoming college students and new employees are expected to know where to find information, how to use it, and, perhaps most important, how to work with people across vast distances in solving problems and making rational decisions. As educators, it is our obligation to ensure that we are offering students every resource available to help them become successful in a future that knows no boundaries.

Resources for Book Study

To help you and your community make the transition to an inquiry-based, multitext school—or to enhance your work if you've already started—you may wish to refer to the following books for guidance.

Literacy Tools in the Classroom: Teaching Through Critical Inquiry, Grades 5–12 by R. Beach, G. Campano, B. Edmiston, and M. Borgmann

Making Thinking Visible: How to Promote Engagement, Understanding, and Independence for All Learners by R. Ritchhart, M. Church, and K. Morrison

Powerful Learning: What We Know About Teaching for Understanding by L. Darling-Hammond and others

21st Century Skills: Rethinking How Students Learn by J. Bellanca and R. Brandt

APPENDIX A
Book Study Essentials

Unlike an Oprah book study in which everyone reads the same book and then talks about it, many professional book studies begin with a question. To address the question, the group identifies and reads a relevant book on the topic and uses information to improve practices in the classroom. I like to think of professional book study as *active* book study. For example, if teachers feel that they are not sufficiently differentiating instruction for their students, they may want to read one of Carol Ann Tomlinson's books on the topic. As they read each chapter, they can try suggested activities with their students and return to the next session with a report about how things went. They may bring video, student work samples, or observational notes to make the discussion relevant.

Here are some tips to help ensure book study success:

- Rotate the position of facilitator so that everyone has a chance to lead the discussion.
- Set ground rules at the onset of the book study, such as "Our meetings will never exceed one hour."
- Require that all teachers report on a practice or strategy that they used from the book and that they bring student work samples from the lesson to share.
- Make readings a reasonable number of pages—divide long chapters into sections.
- Set up a blog so that participants can communicate with each other between sessions.
- Avoid assessment practices, such as having teachers answer questions about what they have read.
- Find a way for teachers to observe each other or co-teach when trying out new activities.

APPENDIX B

Lesson Study Essentials

Lesson study has been used successfully in Japan for many years. It is a process whereby teachers in grade-level or content-area groups work together to plan, observe, analyze, and refine classroom lessons, often called "research lessons." Teachers meet over long periods of time to work on the design, implementation, assessment, and improvement of these lessons. An important part of lesson study is that teachers observe the lesson as one teacher is conducting it, and then meet to discuss how the lesson can be improved.

The following steps can help you organize lesson study within your community.

1. The group members will define a problem or issue that they have identified from their own practices, such as "How can we help students improve vocabulary skills?"
2. All group members participate in planning a lesson, such as a vocabulary lesson. Teachers often use professional resources, such as a book or article (or the chapter on vocabulary in this book), before planning the lesson. "The goal is not only to produce an effective lesson but also to understand why and how the lesson works to promote understanding among students" (Stigler & Hiebert, 1999, p. 113).
3. After the group develops the lesson, choose one teacher to teach the lesson.
4. The other members of the group will observe while the lesson is being taught. Often the lesson is filmed. It is important to note that the focus is on the lesson, not the teacher. For example, observers often watch student responses to the lesson to learn about its effectiveness. Group members may want to read about "ethnographic research" to help them become objective observers.

5. The group will then evaluate the lesson. For example, which aspects of the lesson were most effective? In what way? Which aspects of the lesson need additional development? What were students' responses to each part of the lesson?

6. As a group, the teachers make decisions about how to revise the lesson, based on their observations. They may change such things as the focus of the lesson, the materials, or even the arrangement of the room.

7. A different teacher is chosen to present the revised lesson to a different class. In some cases, the entire department, team, or whole school is invited to observe the lesson.

8. Everyone who observed the lesson participates in an evaluation of the lesson. Sometimes a consultant will be brought in to help refine understandings.

9. Share the results in a report or article, on a website, or even in a published book.

APPENDIX C
Action Research Essentials

Action research is much like lesson study, but it pinpoints a specific challenge or practice in an effort to determine its effectiveness. It is a process that allows you to determine if what you are doing works. Teachers in their communities collaborate in evaluating a practice jointly. For example, your team's strategy might have been for students to use vocabulary words in sentences as a way to help them come to understand meanings, but students don't seem to have conceptual understandings of the words. For example, here's a process for engaging in an action research project on this problem.

1. Problem identification. Often the problem is stated in the form of a research question after the group brainstorms all aspects of the issue. In the above example, the problem would be that students don't understand key vocabulary. The research question might be "What vocabulary practices will help students understand word meanings?"
2. Data collection. Before you form a plan for resolving the vocabulary issue, you will want to collect data to see if you can pinpoint the problem. The data may be informal, perhaps from student surveys or teacher observations, and you may include formal data as well, such as test scores.
3. Data analysis. Your group will study the data to see if you can gain any new understandings or patterns from the data. Maybe you will discover that students aren't fully explaining the words when they use them in sentences. In addition, you may have found that test scores increase when you allow students to discuss words in groups.
4. Plan for action. What is your group going to do differently as a result of your research? Perhaps you will divide vocabulary activities

among members in an effort to determine which activity seems to help students with vocabulary.

5. Report results. In this step, just as in lesson study, groups report their findings to the entire faculty so that everyone can benefit from the research. Groups may also wish to publish their findings.

With a little practice, your group will be ready to adapt the process to your own action research problem.

APPENDIX D
Co-Teaching Essentials

Co-teaching is one of the best ways to incorporate new practices, tap into the collective knowledge of teachers, and ignite renewed enthusiasm for teaching and learning. There is no formula for creating an effective co-teaching team because it relies on the unique, synergistic process based on the personalities of the teachers. In its simplest form, two teachers from the same or different disciplines come together to teach a common group of students. The teachers work out scheduling logistics and plan how they will teach lessons together. As states, districts, and schools implement Common Core State Standards, co-teaching will become even more important because teachers will need the support and insight of their peers to make significant changes in their practices. Following are some tips for making this process work smoothly.

- Teachers work best together when they have a similar philosophy of teaching. For example, a strict disciplinarian who insists that students stay relatively quiet would probably find it difficult to co-teach with someone who loves to incorporate hands-on, collaborative activities with students in groups.
- Think outside the box in terms of scheduling and class arrangements. For example, a high school social studies teacher and an English teacher on the block schedule can offer students a full credit in both subjects by keeping the same group of students for 90 minutes each day for the entire school year instead of only one semester. Seventh and eighth grade science teachers may bring classes together for common labs or blend the classes for two years and teach together.
- Co-teachers need flexibility in curriculum, pacing, and resources to make this endeavor successful. If math and science

teachers team-teach, for example, they may decide to devote several days only to math (or to science) depending on the topic of study.

- Make sure the team teachers have common planning periods and a quiet space in which to plan.
- Both teachers should always remain in the room during the class even if one is the lead teacher for a particular topic. The idea is that two teachers, working together, will be able to support learning for students better than one teacher alone.

References

Allen, J. (2007). *Inside words: Tools for teaching academic vocabulary, grades 4–12.* Portland, ME: Stenhouse.

Allington, R. (2002, November). You can't learn much from books you can't read. *Educational Leadership, 60*(3), 16–19.

Alvermann, D. E. (2003). Seeing themselves as capable and engaged readers: Adolescents and re/mediated instruction. Retrieved from http://www.learningpt.org/pdfs/literacy/readers.pdf.

Anders, P. L., & Spitler, E. (2007). Reinventing comprehension instruction for adolescents. In J. Lewis & G. Moorman (Eds.), *Adolescent literacy instruction: Policies and promising practices* (pp. 167–191). Newark, DE: International Reading Association.

Angelou, M. (1983). *I know why the caged bird sings.* New York: Random.

Angelou, M. (1993). *Life doesn't frighten me.* New York: Stewart, Tabori, & Chang.

Bardoe, C. (2006). *Gregor Mendel: The friar who grew peas.* New York: Harry N. Abrams.

Barell, J. (2003). *Developing more curious minds.* Alexandria, VA: ASCD.

Barell, J. (2010). Problem–based learning: The foundation for 21st century skills. In J. Bellanca & R. Brandt (Eds.), *21st century skills: Rethinking how students learn* (pp. 179–199). Bloomington, IN: Solution Tree.

Barron, B., & Darling-Hammond, L. (2008). How can we teach for meaningful learning? In L. Darling-Hammond (Ed.), *Powerful learning: What we know about teaching for understanding* (pp. 11–70). San Francisco: Jossey-Bass.

Beck, I. L., McKeown, M. G., & Kucan, L. (2002). *Bringing words to life: Robust vocabulary instruction.* New York: The Guilford Press.

Birnbaum, M. (2010). Historians speak out against proposed Texas textbook changes. *The Washington Post.* Retrieved from http://washingtonpost.com/wp–dyn/content/article/2010/03/17/AR2010031700560.html.

Black, P., & Wiliam, D. (1998). Inside the black box: Raising standards through classroom assessment. *Phi Delta Kappan.* Retrieved from http://blog.discoveryeducation.com/assessment/files/2009/02/blackbox_article.pdf.

Brozo, W. G., Shiel, G., & Topping, K. (2007). Engagement in reading: Lessons learned from three PISA countries. *Journal of Adolescent and Adult Literacy. 51*(4), 304–315.

Bryant, J. (2008). *A river of words: The story of William Carlos Williams.* Grand Rapids, MI: Eerdsman's Books for Young Readers.

Buehl, D. (2001). *Classroom strategies for interactive learning* (2nd ed.). Newark, DE: International Reading Association.

Bunting, E. (1992). *The wall.* New York: Clarion.

Calkins, L., Ehrenworth, M., & Lehman, C. (2012). *Pathways to the common core: Accelerating achievement.* Portsmouth, NH: Heinemann.

Cambourne, B. (1988). *The whole story: Natural learning and the acquisition of literacy in the classroom.* New York: Scholastic.

Carr, E., & Wixson, K. K. (1986, April). Guidelines for evaluating vocabulary instruction. *Journal of Reading, 29*(7), 588–595.

Carr, K., Buchannan, D., Wentz, J., Weiss, M., & Brant, K. (2001). Not just for the primary grades: A bibliography of picture books for secondary content teachers. *Journal of Adolescent and Adult Literacy, 45*(2), 146–153.

Collins, A., & Halverson, R. (2009). *Rethinking education in the age of technology: The digital revolution and schooling in America.* New York: Teachers College Press.

Connecticut Association of Schools. (2008). *Moving toward secondary school reform: Programs to engage seniors.* Retrieved from http://www.casciac.org/pdfs/Moving_Toward_Secondary_School_Reform.pdf.

Cooney, C. (2007). *Code orange.* New York: Laurel-Leaf.

Copeland, L. (2009). Cherokee reunion celebrates heritage. *USA Today.* Retrieved from www.usatoday.com/news/nation/2009–04–16–Cherokee_N.htm.

Danticat, E., Na, A., Yep, L., & others. (2012). Research and discovery. [Online workshop; Teaching multicultural literature: A workshop for the middle grades]. Available from http://www.learner.org/workshops/tml/workshop4/teaching.html.

Darling-Hammond, L. (2010a). *The flat world and education: How America's commitment to equity will determine our future.* New York: Teachers College Press.

Darling-Hammond, L. (2010b). New policies for 21st century demands. In J. Bellanca & R. Brandt (Eds.). *21st century skills: Rethinking how students learn* (pp. 32–49). Bloomington, IN: Solution Tree.

Darling-Hammond, L., Barron, B., Pearson, P. D., Schoenfeld, A. H., Stage, E. K., Zimmerman, T. D., Cervetti, G. N., & Tilson, J. L. (2008). *Powerful learning: What we know about teaching for understanding.* San Francisco: Jossey-Bass.

Dekker, T. (2011). *Blink of an eye.* New York: Center Street Press.

Dilworth, T. (1798). *The schoolmaster's assistant, being a compendium of arithmetic both practical and theoretical.* Glasgow: J. & A. Duncan.

Douglass, J. E., & Guthrie, J. T. (2008). Meaning is motivating: Classroom goal structures. In J. T. Guthrie (Ed.), *Engaging adolescents in reading* (pp. 17–31). Thousand Oaks: Corwin.

Dozier, C., Johnston, P., & Rogers, R. (2006). *Critical literacy/critical teaching.* New York: Teachers College Press.

Effective Grading Practices. (November 2011). *Educational Leadership, 69*(3).

Einhorn, E. (2008). *A very improbable story.* Watertown, MA: Charlesbridge Publishing.

Ellis, J. (2010). *Pythagoras and the ratios: A math adventure.* Watertown, MA: Charlesbridge Publishing.

Feldman, D. (2005). *When do fish sleep and other imponderables of everyday life.* New York: Harper Perennial.

Fillman, S., & Guthrie, J. T. (2008). Control and choice: Supporting self–directed reading. In J. T. Guthrie (Ed.), *Engaging adolescents in reading,* pp. 33–48. Thousand Oaks: Corwin.

Fisher, D., & Frey, N. (2007). *Checking for understanding: Formative assessment techniques for your classroom.* Alexandria, VA: ASCD.

Fisher, D., & Frey, N. (2008). *Word-wise and content rich: Five essential steps to teaching academic vocabulary.* Portsmouth, NH: Heinemann.

Flanigan, R. L. (2012). U.S. schools forge foreign connections via web. *Education Week.* Retrieved from http://www.edweek.org/ew/articles/2012/01/23/19el–globallearning.h31.html.

Frank, A. (2010). *Diary of a young girl.* New York: Everyman's Library.

Frayer, D., Frederick, W. C., & Klausmeier, H. J. (1969). *A schema for testing the level of cognitive mastery.* Madison, WI: Wisconsin Center for Education Research.

Fresch, M. J., & Harkins, P. (2009). *The power of picture books: Using content-area literature in middle school.* Urbana, IL: National Council of Teachers of English.

Fullan, M. (2007). *The new meaning of educational change* (4th ed.). New York: Teachers College Press.

Fulton, K., Yoon, I., & Lee, C. (2005). Induction into learning communities. Retrieved from http://nctaf.org/wp–content/uploads/2012/01/NCTAF_Induction_Paper_2005.pdf.

Fulwiler, B. R. (2011). *Writing in science in action: Strategies, tools, and classroom video.* Portsmouth, NH: Heinemann.

Gallagher, K. (2009). *Readicide: How schools are killing reading and what you can do about it.* Portland, ME: Stenhouse.

Glencoe. (2004). *Biology: The dynamics of life.* Columbus, OH: Glencoe/McGraw-Hill.

Graham, S., & Perin, D. (2007). *Writing next: Effective strategies to improve writing of adolescents in middle and high schools.* [Report to Carnegie Corporation of New York.] Washington, DC: Alliance for Excellent Education.

Graves, M. F. (2005). *The vocabulary book: Learning and instruction.* New York: Teachers College Press.

Guthrie, J. T. (Ed). (2008). *Engaging adolescents in reading.* Thousand Oaks: Corwin.

Guthrie, J. T., & Wigfield, A. (2000). Engagement and motivation in reading. In M. L. Kamil, P. B. Mosenthal, P. D. Pearson, & R. Barr (Eds.), *Handbook of reading research: Volume III* (pp. 403–422). Mahwah, NJ: Erlbaum.

Hadden, M. (2004). *The curious incident of the dog in the night-time.* New York: Vintage.

Hammond, D. W., & Nessel, D. D. (2011). *The comprehension experience: Engaging readers through effective inquiry and discussion.* Portsmouth, NH: Heinemann.

Harcourt School Publishers. (2009). *Forces and motion.* Science student ed., grade 4. Orlando, FL: Author.

Harvey, S., & Daniels, H. (2009). *Comprehension and collaboration: Inquiry circles in collaboration.* Portsmouth, NH: Heinemann.

Harvey, S., & Goudvis, A. (2007). *Strategies that work for understanding and engagement.* Portland, ME: Stenhouse.

Hicks, T. (2009). *The digital writing workshop.* Portsmouth, NH: Heinemann.

Hobbs, W. (2006). *Crossing the wire.* New York: HarperCollins.

Hoose, P. M. (2010). *Claudette Colvin: Twice toward justice.* New York: Square Fish Publishing.

Jackson, Y. (2011). The trouble with professional development for teachers. Retrieved from http://www.washingtonpost.com/blogs/answer–sheet/post/the–trouble–with–professional–development–for–teachers/2011/06/30/AGRxQfrH_blog.html.

Johnson, R. L. (2010). *Journey into the deep: Discovering new ocean creatures.* Minneapolis, MN: Millbrook Press.

Johnson, R. T., & Johnson, D. W. (1986). Action research: Cooperative learning in the science classroom. *Science & Children 24,* 31–32.

Knight, M. B. (2003). *Who belongs here? An American story.* Gardiner, ME: Tilbury House.

Laird, E. (2006). *A little piece of ground.* Chicago: Haymarket Books.

Lane, B. (2008). *But how do you teach writing? A simple guide for all teachers.* New York: Scholastic.

Langer, J. (2010). *Envisioning knowledge: Building literacy in the academic disciplines.* New York: Teachers College Press.

Langer, J. A., & Applebee, A. N. (2007). *How writing shapes thinking: A study of teaching and learning.* [WAC Clearinghouse Landmark Publications in Writing Studies.] Retrieved from http://wac.colostate.edu/books/langer_applebee.

Lenski, S. (2011, Dec.–2012, Jan.). What RTI means for content area teachers. *Journal of Adolescent and Adult Literacy, 55*(4), 276–282.

Lent, R. C. (2009). *Literacy for real: Reading, thinking, and learning in the content areas.* New York: Teachers College Press.

Levinson, C. (2012). *We've got a job: The 1963 Birmingham children's march.* Atlanta: Peachtree Publishers.

Levitt, S. D., & Dubner, S. J. (2009). *Freakonomics: A rogue economist explores the hidden side of everything.* New York: William Morrow.

Lyman, F. T. (1981). The responsive classroom discussion: The inclusion of all students. In A. Anderson (Ed.), *Mainstreaming Digest* (pp. 109–113). College Park: University of Maryland Press.

Mansfield News Journal. (2011). Teacher takes students around the world through technology. *Mansfield News Journal.* Retrieved from http://www.mansfieldnewsjournal.com/fdcp/?unique=1323975921512 accessed 12/15/2011.

Marcarelli, K. (2010). *Teaching science with interactive notebooks.* Thousand Oaks: Corwin.

Marrin, A. (2011). *Flesh and blood so cheap: The triangle fire and its legacy.* New York: Knopf Books for Young Readers.

Marzano, R. J. (2004). *Building background knowledge for academic achievement: Research on what works in schools.* Alexandria, VA: ASCD.

Marzano, R. J., & Pickering, D. J. (2005). *Building academic vocabulary: Teacher's manual.* Alexandria, VA: ASCD.

Masoff, J. (2000). *Oh, yuck! The encyclopedia of everything nasty.* New York: Workman Publishing Co.

Masoff, J. (2006). *Oh, yikes! History's grossest, wackiest moments.* New York: Workman Publishing Co.

McGraw-Hill/Glencoe. (2007). *Focus on life science,* p. 479 [El Niño], p. 320 [volcanoes]. Columbus, OH: Author.

McKinley, J. C., Jr. (March 12, 2010). Texas conservatives win curriculum change. *New York Times.* Retrieved from http://www.nytimes.com/2010/03/13/education/13texas.html.

McTighe, J., & Seif, E. (2010). An implementation framework to support 21st century skills. In J. Bellanca and R. Brandt (Eds.), *21st century skills: Rethinking how students learn,* pp. 149–172. Bloomington, IN: Solution Tree.

Myers, W. D. (2005). *Patrol: An American soldier in Vietnam.* New York: HarperCollins.

Nagy, W. E. (1988). *Teaching vocabulary to improve reading comprehension.* Newark, DE: International Reading Association.

National Commission on Writing for America's Families, Schools, and Colleges. (2006, May). *Writing and school reform, including the neglected "R": The need for a writing revolution.* (Report.) Retrieved from http://www.collegeboard.com/prod_downloads/writingcom/writing-school-reform-natl-comm-writing.pdf.

National Council of Teachers of English. (2008). *Writing now.* [Policy research brief.] Retrieved from http://www.ncte.org/library/NCTEFiles/Resources/PolicyResearch/WrtgResearchBrief.pdf.

National Council of Teachers of English. (2011). *Communities of Practice: A Policy Research Brief.* Retrieved from http://www.ncte.org/library/NCTEFiles/Resources/Journals/CC/0212nov2011/CC0212Policy.pdf.

National Research Council. (2000). *How people learn: Brain, mind, experience, and school* (Expanded ed.). Washington DC: National Academy Press.

National Writing Project & Nagin, C. (2006). *Because writing matters: Improving student writing in our schools* (Rev. ed.). San Francisco: Jossey-Bass.

Neil, M. (2003). The dangers of testing. *Educational Leadership, 60*(5), 43–46.

Neuschwander, C. (2004). *Sir Cumference and the dragon of pi: A math adventure* [series]. Watertown, MA: Charlesbridge Publishing.

Organisation for Economic Co-operation and Development (OECD). (2011). *Education at a glance 2011: OECD indicators.* Retrieved from http://www.oecd.org/document/2/0,3746,en_2649_39263238_48634114_1_1_1_1,00.html.

Orwell, G. (2003). *Animal farm.* New York: Plume.

Orwell, G. (2009). *Facing unpleasant facts: Narrative essays.* New York: Mariner Books.

Palmer, K. (2012). Budding writers benefit from sharing their work online. Retrieved from http://blogs.kqed.org/mindshift/2012/04/budding-writers-benefit-from-sharing-their-work-online.

Pearson, D. (2010, July). "Still time for a change." Speech presented at IRA World Congress in Aukland, New Zealand.

Pink, D. H. (2011). *Drive: The surprising truth about what motivates us.* New York: Riverhead Books.

Rather, D. (2012, April 3). Finnish first. (Dan Rather Reports.) Available from http://www.hd.net/programs/danrather.

Reeves, D. (2007). *Ahead of the curve: The power of assessment to transform teaching and learning.* Bloomington, IN: Solution Tree.

Restak, R. (2003). *The new brain: How the modern age is rewiring your mind.* Emmaus, PA: Rodale.

Richtel, M. (2012, Jan. 20). Blogs vs. term papers. Retrieved from http://www.nytimes.com/2012/01/22/education/edlife/muscling-in-on-the-term-paper-tradition.html.

Rinaldi, A. (1995). *The secret of Sarah Revere.* Orlando, FL: Gulliver Books/Harcourt.

Roseth, C. J., Johnson, D. W., & Johnson, R. T. (2008, March). Promoting early adolescents' achievement and peer relationships: The effects of cooperative, competitive, and individualistic goal structures. *Psychological Bulletin, 134*(2), 223–246.

Rushton, S., & Juola–Rushton, A. M. (2007). Performance assessment in the elementary grades. In P. Jones, J. Carr, & R. Ataya (Eds.), *A pig don't get fatter the more you weigh it: Classroom assessments that work* (pp. 29–38). New York: Teachers College Press.

Schallert, D. (2002). Schema theory. In B. J. Guzzetti (Ed.), *Literacy in America: An encyclopedia of history, theory and practice* (pp. 556–558). Santa Barbara, CA: ABC-CLIO.

Schanzer, R. (2007). *George vs George: The American revolution as seen from both sides.* Des Moines, IA: National Geographic Children's Books.

Schmoker, M. (2010, Sept. 27). When pedagogic fads trump priorities. *Education Week.* Retrieved from http://www.edweek.org/ew/articles/2010/09/29/05schmoker.h30.html.

Schoenfeld, A. H. (2008). Mathematics for understanding. In L. Darling-Hammond, et al. (Eds.), *Powerful learning: What we know about teaching for understanding* (pp. 113–150). San Francisco: Jossey–Bass.

Schunk, D. H. (2003). Self-efficacy for reading and writing: Influence of modeling, goal setting, and self-evaulation. *Reading and Writing Quarterly: Overcoming Learning Difficulties 19,* 159–172.

Science Illustrated contributors. (2011, Sept./Oct.). Are some volcanoes more dangerous than others? *Science Illustrated,* p. 22. Retrieved from http://www.scienceillustrated.com/nature/2011/08/are–some–volcanoes–more–dangerous–others.

Sewell, A. (2011). *Black Beauty.* Hollywood, FL: Simon & Brown.

Steinbeck, J. (2002). *Of mice and men.* New York: Penguin.

Stiggins, R. (2002, June). Assessment crisis: The absence of assessment for learning. *Phi Delta Kappan, 83*(10), 758–765. Retrieved from http://www.pdkintl.org/kappan/k0206sti.htm.

Stigler, J. W., & Hiebert, J. (1999). *The teaching gap: Best ideas from the world's teachers for improving education in the classroom.* New York: Free Press.

Tharoor, I. (2010, Oct. 25). Military parades. *Time,* p. 35.

Tovani, C. (2011). It's not too late to be smart: The hope and how of secondary strategies instruction. In H. Daniels (Ed.), *Comprehension going forward: Where we are and what's next* (pp. 174–191). Portsmouth, NH: Heinemann.

Vacca, R. T., & Mraz, M. (2011). Content–area reading instruction. In T. V. Rasinski (Ed.). *Rebuilding the foundation: Effective reading instruction for 21st century literacy.* Bloomington, IN: Solution Tree Press.

Volante, L. (2004, Sept. 25). Teaching to the test: What every educator and policy–maker should know. *Canadian Journal of Educational Administration and Policy,* (35).

Von Drehle, D. (2008, June 30). A new line in the sand. *Time, 171*(26), 36–38.

Von Drehle, D. (2010, Oct. 4). This really sucks. *Time, 176*(14), 36–38.

Wentzel, K. (1998). Social relationships and motivation in middle school: The role of parents, teachers, and peers. *Journal of Educational Psychology, 90,* 202–209.

Wiggins, G., & McTighe, J. (1998). *Understanding by design.* Alexandria, VA: ASCD.

Wilhelm, J. (2007). *Engaging readers and writers with inquiry: Promoting deep understandings in language arts and the content areas with guiding questions.* New York: Scholastic.

Williams-Garcia, R. (2011). *One crazy summer.* New York: Amistad.

Wolk, S. (2008, Oct.). School as inquiry. *Phi Delta Kappan, 90*(2), 115–122.

Wormeli, R. (2011, Nov.) Redos and retakes done right. *Educational Leadership, 69*(3), 22–26.

Zakaria, F. (2011). How U.S. graduation rates compare with the rest of the world. Retrieved from http://globalpublicsquare.blogs.cnn.com/2011/11/03/how-u-s-graduation-rates-compare with-the-rest-of-the-world/.

Zenatti, V. (2008). *A bottle in the Gaza sea.* New York: Bloomsbury USA Children's Publishing.

Index

The letter *f* following a page number denotes a figure.

About the Author

ReLeah Cossett Lent was a teacher for more than 20 years before becoming a founding member of a statewide literacy project at the University of Central Florida. She is now an international education consultant. Lent writes, speaks, and provides workshops on topics ranging from literacy to creating communities of practice within schools and districts.

Lent's first two books, co-authored with Gloria Pipkin and published by Heinemann, *At the Schoolhouse Gate: Lessons in Intellectual Freedom* and *Silent No More: Stories of Courage in American Schools,* won the American Library Association's Intellectual Freedom Award and the NCTE/Slate Intellectual Freedom Award. Lent also received the PEN/Newman's Own First Amendment Award in 1999.

She has been published in professional journals and has written several books, including *Adolescents on the Edge, Stories and Lessons to Transform Learning* with DVD, co-authored with Jimmy Santiago Baca (Heinemann, 2010); *Literacy for Real:*

Reading, Thinking, and Learning in the Content Areas (Teachers College Press, 2009); *Literacy Learning Communities: A Guide for Creating Sustainable Change in Secondary Schools* (Heinemann, 2007); and *Engaging Adolescent Learners: A Guide for Content-Area Teachers* (Heinemann, 2006). Lent's most recent publication is *Keep Them Reading: Avoiding Challenges and Censorship* (Teachers College Press, 2012).

Lent may be reached at rlent@tds.net.

Related ASCD Resources: Learning and Literacy in the Content Areas and Communities of Learning

At the time of publication, the following ASCD resources were available (ASCD stock numbers appear in parentheses). For up-to-date information about ASCD resources, go to www.ascd.org.

Professional Interest Communities

Visit the ASCD Website (www.ascd.org) and scroll to the bottom to click on "professional interest communities." Within these communities, find information about professional educators who have formed groups around topics like "Literacy, Language, and Literature," "Professional Learning Communities," and "Interdisciplinary Curriculum and Instruction."

ASCD EDge Group

Exchange ideas and connect with other educators interested in various topics, including Engagement & School Completion or Action Research and PLCs on the social networking site ASCD EDge™ at http://ascdedge.ascd.org/

PD Online

Common Core and Literacy Strategies: Science
Common Core and Literacy Strategies: History/Social Studies
Common Core and Literacy Strategies: Mathematics
Common Core and Literacy Strategies: English Language Arts
These and other online courses are available at www.ascd.org/pdonline

Print Products

Assignments Matter: Making the Connections That Help Students Meet Standards by Eleanor Dougherty (#112048)

Building Literacy in Social Studies: Strategies for Improving Comprehension and Critical Thinking by Donna Ogle, Ron M. Klemp, and Bill McBride (#106010)

Effective Literacy Coaching: Building Expertise and a Culture of Literacy: An ASCD Action Tool by Shari Frost, Roberta Buhle, and Camille Blachowicz (#109044)

The Fundamentals of Literacy Coaching by Amy Sandvold and Maelou Baxter (#107084)

Literacy Leadership for Grades 5–12 by Rosemarye Taylor and Valerie Doyle Collins (#103022)

Literacy Strategies for Improving Mathematics Instruction by Joan M. Kenney, Euthecia A. Hancewicz, Loretta Heuer, Diana Metsisto, and Cynthia L. Tuttle (#105137)

Protocols for Professional Learning by Lois Brown Easton (#109037)

Reading for Meaning: How to Build Students' Comprehension, Reasoning, and Problem-Solving Skills by Harvey F. Silver, Susan C. Morris, and Victor Klein (#110128)

Strengthening and Enriching Your Professional Learning Community: The Art of Learning Together by Geoffrey Caine and Renate N. Caine (#110085)

Teaching Reading in the Content Areas: If Not Me, Then Who? 3rd edition by Vicki Urquhart and Dana J. Frazee (#112024)

Understanding Common Core State Standards by John Kendall (#112011)

THE WHOLE CHILD The Whole Child Initiative helps schools and communities create learning environments that allow students to be healthy, safe, engaged, supported, and challenged. To learn more about other books and resources that relate to the whole child, visit www.wholechildeducation.org.

For more information: send e-mail to member@ascd.org; call 1-800-933-2723 or 703-578-9600, press 2; send a fax to 703-575-5400; or write to Information Services, ASCD, 1703 N. Beauregard St., Alexandria, VA 22311-1714 USA.